D0967026

THE *LITTLE BOOK OF LORE* FOR

DOG
LOVERS

THE LITTLE BOOK OF LORE FOR

DOG LOVERS

A COMPENDIUM OF DOGGONE
FACTS, HISTORY, AND LEGEND

MARY FRANCES BUDZIK

Skyhorse Publishing

First Skyhorse Publishing edition
© Toucan Books Ltd. 2021

Skyhorse Publishing books may be purchased in bulk at special discounts for sales promotion, corporate gifts, fund-raising, or educational purposes. Special editions can also be created to specifications. For details, contact the Special Sales Department, Skyhorse Publishing, 307 West 36th Street, 11th Floor, New York, NY 10018 or info@skyhorsepublishing.com.

Skyhorse® and Skyhorse Publishing® are registered trademarks of Skyhorse Publishing, Inc.®, a Delaware corporation.

Visit our website at www.skyhorsepublishing.com.

10 9 8 7 6 5 4 3 2 1

Library of Congress Cataloging-in-Publication Data is available on file.

Cover design by Daniel Brount
Cover illustration from Getty images

Print ISBN: 978-1-5107-6288-6
Ebook ISBN: 978-1-5107-6290-9

Printed in China

CONTENTS

CHAPTER 1

The Dog

It can be easy to forget that the dog who looms so large in the back of your SUV, at the foot of your bed—and in your checkbook!—is the descendant of a wolf. Over the centuries, the canine has been domesticated and evolved into a kaleidoscope of breeds, all bred for specific traits. Yet all dogs, from the imposing Doberman pinscher to the diminutive Maltese terrier, purebred or mutt, have the same common ancestor: the wolf.

MAN AND DOG

The study of dogs is known as "cynology," from *kyon,* the Greek word for "dog," and *logos,* or "knowledge." The Greek word *kynikos,* from which cynic comes, meant "doglike." The word was probably applied to the Cynic philosophers because the epithet Kyon was hurled at Diogenes of Sinope, an Athenian beggar and the prototypical Cynic. Diogenes praised the virtues of dogs, who lived and mated on the street and were not self-conscious about bodily functions. He advocated the simplicities of self-sufficiency and shamelessness—all he claimed to find in the dog.

The Canid family includes all dogs—wild, domestic, and extinct. The DNA of dogs and gray wolves is nearly identical. Most researchers believe wolves evolved when they were domesticated about 15,000 years ago. However, some researchers believe that dogs diverged from wolves even earlier—100,000 years ago.

In the course of the evolution from wolves to dogs, the domestic dog ended up with a smaller skull than the wolf (less brain room), less sensory area, and smaller teeth crowded into a smaller jaw.

Dr. Peter Savolainen, a Swedish researcher, collected DNA of 654 dogs from around the world. His analysis suggests that dogs derived from a family tree of just three wolves, 15,000 years ago in Asia, and spread westward. Genetic tests of South American dog fossils show that they are genetically linked to the Asian dogs, suggesting that the dogs of the Americas migrated here with "their" people from Asia.

THEORIES OF CANINE DOMESTICATION

The traditional scenario of canine domestication pictures a dominant cave man rescuing a litter of orphaned wolf puppies and, in a gesture curiously magnanimous for a subsistence hunter-gatherer, raising them as his own. Voila, domestication. However, most researchers now believe that dogs domesticated themselves, at least 15,000 years ago, when early man first began to settle down and live in settled encampments. Wolves lingered at the edges of human encampments and scavenged bones, scraps, and even sewage. Eventually, those wolves that could tolerate the proximity of people and eat in the vicinity of humans became part of the customary fabric of early human life.

Researchers point out that the social systems of dog and man complement each other, and that while dogs gained greater access to food and perhaps comfort and protection in the presence of man, men gained alarm systems, guards, hunting companions (as social hunters living in groups, their hunting styles may have been compatible), perhaps an emergency food supply, and, eventually, bed warmers and boon companions!

🐾 Dr. Raymond Coppinger of Hampshire College in Massachusetts theorizes that wolves with a shorter "flight distance" had an evolutionary advantage (they had better access to food) and eventually developed with a different biochemistry from wolves, evolving into canis familiaris—the dog—instead of remaining as *canis lupus*—the wolf.

🐾 A Russian study on foxes bred solely for tameability found that over the course of generations, the tameable foxes selected developed certain traits, such as floppy ears, piebald or mottled coat patterns, and shorter muzzles, although the foxes chosen for breeding were selected solely for their ability to be tamed, not for any physical trait.

> *Dogs watch for us faithfully: they love and worship their masters . . .*
> CICERO 106–43 B.C., ROMAN ORATOR

DOGS OF ALL SHAPES AND SIZES

Dogs exhibit the greatest variation in size of any single mammalian species. To analyze why, researchers studied the DNA of the Portuguese water dog, a breed that shows a great variation in skeletal size. Researchers discovered that there was a variant on the insulin growth factor 1 (IGF1) gene between the large and small Portuguese water dogs. The study was then extended to analyze the DNA of over 3,200 dogs. The material was obtained from the database of the Mars candy company, which also makes pet food and which maintains the largest gene bank of canine DNA in the world! The analysis confirmed that size variation among dog breeds is controlled by a single variant on the IGF1 gene; small dogs have the variant and large dogs do not.

RECORD BREAKERS

CHLOE, TIBETAN MASTIFF: 365 pounds (165 kg), 38 inches (96.5 cm) tall at shoulder; 8 feet 5 inches (2.6 m) nose to tail tip.

GIBSON, HARLEQUIN GREAT DANE: about 42 inches (107 cm) at the shoulder; nearly 7 feet (2.1 m) tall on his hind legs.

DANCER, CHIHUAHUA: just over 4 inches (10 cm) tall at the shoulder, weighing only 18 ounces (510 g).

SYLVIA, YORKSHIRE TERRIER: Smallest dog ever recorded at 2½ inches (6.35 cm) tall, 3½ inches (8.9 cm) long, and weighing 4 ounces (113 g).

RECORD-BREAKING DOG BREEDS

HEAVIEST DOGS (AVERAGE WEIGHT OF MALE DOGS)

English mastiff	175–220 lb.	(80–100 kg)
Saint Bernard	110–200 lb.	(50–90 kg)
Neapolitan mastiff	150–170 lb.	(70–80 kg)
Newfoundland	130–150 lb.	(60–70 kg)
Irish wolfhound	150–200 lb.	(70–90 kg)

SMALLEST DOGS (MAXIMUM WEIGHT)

Chihuahua	6 lb.	(2.7 kg)
Yorkshire terrier	7 lb.	(3 kg)
Maltese	7 lb.	(3 kg)
Pomeranian	7 lb.	(3 kg)
Silky terrier (*no official maximum*)	10 lb.	(4.5 kg)
Brussels Griffon	12 lb.	(5.4 kg)

TALLEST DOGS (MINIMUM HEIGHT OF MALE DOGS)

Irish wolfhound	32 in.	(81 cm)
Great Dane	30 in.	(76 cm
English mastiff	30 in.	(76 cm
Anatolian shepherd dog	29 in.	(74 cm)
Borzoi	28 in.	(71 cm)
Saint Bernard	27½ in.	(70 cm)

SHORTEST DOGS (MAXIMUM HEIGHT)

Chihuahua (*no official maximum*)	8 in.	(20 cm)
Brussels griffon (*no official maximum*)	8 in.	(20 cm)
Yorkshire terrier (*no official maximum*)	9 in.	(23 cm)
Maltese (*no official maximum*)	10 in.	(25 cm)
Silky terrier	10 in.	(25 cm)
Shih tzu	10½ in.	(26.5 cm)

EQUIPPED FOR SURVIVAL

Have you ever watched a dog intently smelling a patch of ground or pavement and thought that he resembled nothing so much as a wine connoisseur rolling a fine vintage over his palate? That analogy is actually quite descriptive of how the dog "tastes" scent. The canine sense of smell is at least 10,000 times more sensitive than a human's. Canine noses have 220 million scent receptors, in contrast to the human's meager 5 million. The canine sniffer is also perfectly designed to maximize a dog's experience of scent molecules. The moisture of the dog's nose sponges up scent molecules and the slits at the corners of the nostrils flare to circulate the molecules into the inner nasal chamber, which features a "pocket," known as the subethmoidal shelf, that allows scent molecules to accumulate and interact with the plenteous supply of olfactory receptor cells in the dog's nasal epithelium.

The enthusiastic "snuffling" of dogs, and even the long ears of scent hounds, such as the bloodhound and beagle, stir up scent molecules and create a denser "cloud" for the dog to inhale. Even the dog's brain is designed to "compute" the information in scent molecules. The olfactory lobe in the canine brain is highly developed. So now you know why your dog lingers forever over a slab of sidewalk! He is simply reading the doggy equivalent of the daily *New York Times*!

NIGHT VISION

Although dogs don't see color as well as humans, they have a wider field of vision, a better ability to detect motion, and better night vision. Their retinas have fewer cones than humans, but more rods, which are important for night vision. They also have tissue in their eyes that acts like a mirror, reflecting light entering the eyes back through the retina, reactivating the ocular light-sensing cells, and intensifying their signals to the brain.

HIGHS AND LOWS

Dogs can detect sounds (air vibration, measured as frequencies, in hertz) as low as 16 to 20 Hz and as high as above 45 Hz. Their hearing is significantly better than humans at high frequencies and roughly comparable at low frequencies; however, dogs are able to hear sounds of lower intensity (decibels) than humans. Dogs with erect ears have the best hearing. Canines, unlike people, have at least 18 muscles that enable them to move the pinnas (flaps) of their ears to enhance reception and pinpoint the source of a sound—as if they had an old-fashioned ear "trumpet" that they were able to position at will! Ironically, deafness is also quite common in dogs, particularly in dogs with mostly white coats, such as Dalmatians and English bull terriers.

BY A WHISKER

Dog whiskers are touch-sensitive hairs called vibrissae. Located on the muzzle, above the eyes, and below the jaws, they are sensitive to tiny changes in air flow and are connected to an important cranial nerve. Although their precise function in canine sensory perception has not been studied, the show grooming practice of shaving off the vibrissae to give the dog's face a "clean" look has been decried by some as the amputation of an important sensory organ.

CARNASSIAL TEETH

In their upper and lower jaws, dogs have shearing teeth, known as carnassials, that can move through flesh like a scissors in order to rend it from the bone. Little wonder that the "doggie toys" we buy for our modern companions often end up disemboweled!

NO BONES ABOUT IT

A dog's skeleton has 319 bones—that's about 100 more bones than a human. It's probably obvious that the size of the bones varies between breeds; however, the shape of the bones varies, too.

HAVING PUPPIES

If you let your bitch—a female dog—have puppies, here are a few facts. The average time between a bitch's heat periods is six to nine months; heats (or "seasons") last about 21 days. African breeds, such as the Rhodesian ridgeback and the basenji, come into heat yearly, like wild dogs, which have less frequent heats.

"Standing" heat, when the bitch is fertile and receptive to the male, starts about the ninth day and can last to the nineteenth. A bitch signals standing heat by "hussy" behavior; she presents her rear end to the male, and if you touch the base of her tail, she will hold it clamped to the side. During the heat period many bitches bleed; but some bitches can go through "silent" heats (but still be fertile), so be alert for any sign, especially when your bitch is due to come in heat.

Brucellosis, an infectious disease, is a major cause of infertility in both male and female dogs and can be transmitted by breeding. All breeding dogs should have a negative brucellosis test before being bred.

If you do not intend to breed your bitch, have her spayed before her first heat. An intact bitch has a seven times greater risk of developing breast cancer than a bitch spayed before her first heat. Breast cancer is common in older unspayed females and is fatal at least 50 percent of the time. The operation to remove the tumors, even if the bitch survives, is risky and expensive surgery.

FALSE ALARM

Unspayed females, even if they have not been bred, can have a false pregnancy. About six to ten weeks after the heat cycle, hormonal changes can cause the bitch to mother puppylike objects (such as a slipper), build a nest, and even lactate and develop an enlarged abdomen. Most false pregnancies subside on their own, but if your bitch is in a lot of distress, the veterinarian can prescribe hormone treatments. False pregnancy tends to recur; again, it is far easier on everyone concerned, as well as healthier, to spay most bitches!

WHAT TO EXPECT WHEN A DOG IS EXPECTING

The canine gestation period, from the day of conception to birth, is an average of 63 days. Puppies born within 59–66 days are in the normal range; if born earlier than 57 days, the pups may not survive. The canine uterus is a Y-shaped organ; each "horn" of the Y, on either side of the abdomen, carries a series of embryos, like peas in a pod. Palpation for pregnancy is possible from 27 to 35 days after conception; after 35 days, the uterus is too fluid filled. An experienced palpater may be able to estimate the size of the litter by feeling the individual embryos.

BIG LITTERS

The average size of a litter of puppies depends on the breed, with smaller breeds having fewer puppies. Some bitches have been exceptionally prolific:

- Tia, a Neapolitan mastiff, had 24 puppies in 2005.
- Careless Anne (indeed!), a Saint Bernard, gave birth to 23 puppies in 1975.
- An American foxhound had 23 puppies in Ambler, Pennsylvania, in 1944.
- One Great Dane had a truly "great" delivery, with 23 puppies, in 1987.

TIME-TESTED DOG NAMES

Belle	Fido	Patch
Bingo	Jock	Rover
Blue	Lad	Rusty
Buddy	Lady	Spot
Buster	Lassie	Trixie
Duke	Nip	

TOP CONTEMPORARY DOG NAMES

Bailey	Jake	Molly
Bear	Lucky	Rocky
Buddy	Lucy	Shadow
Buster	Maggie	Sam
Daisy	Max	

NOTE: You are more likely to be bitten by a dog named *Rocky* than any one with any other dog name.

DO YOU SPEAK DOG?

CANINE BODY LANGUAGE

	NEUTRAL, CALM	INTERESTED, ALERT	AGGRESSIVE	SUBMISSIVE
Eyes	Soft, interested	Large, staring	Hard, staring	Half closed, may blink, whites may show ("whale eye")
Ears	Naturally erect or relaxed, depending on ear type	Up and forward	Erect and forward	Back, close to head
Tail	Relaxed, gently wagging (in a slow swing)	Up, may wag at an increased tempo	Raised, may wag stiffly	Low, between legs, may wag a bit (the tip)
Body attitude	Normal, not raised or lowered	May pace a bit or stand on tiptoe, may cock head slightly	Stands tall, hackles (erectile hair on the neck, shoulders, root of the tail) up	Lowered, probably curved, possibly trembling
Mouth	Slightly open	Possibly open, but no teeth showing	Lips curled, teeth bared	Closed, tongue may dart out; some dogs grimace and expose just the incisor teeth in a "submissive grin"

HOW TO BARK IN DIFFERENT LANGUAGES!

CANTONESE: Wo! Wo!

CATALAN: Bup! Bup!

CZECH: Haf haf!

DUTCH: Woef! Woef! (big dog) or Waf! Waf! (little dog)

ENGLISH: Woof! Arf! Bow wow! Yip yip! Yap yap (small dogs)!

ESTONIAN: Auh-auh!

FINNISH: Hau hau or Vuh vuh!

FRENCH: Wouaff! Wouaff! or Ouah Ouah

GERMAN: Wau! Wau! (pronounced like "vow") or Wuff! Wuff!

GREEK: Gav! Gav!

HEBREW: Hav hav!

INDONESIAN: Gong! Gong!

ITALIAN: Bau! Bau!

JAPANESE: Wan! Wan!

KOREAN: Mong! Mong!

LEBANESE: Haw! Haw!

MANDARIN (HAN) CHINESE: Wang! Wang!

NIGERIA, CALABAR AREA: Wai! Wai!

NORWEGIAN: Voff! Voff!

POLISH: How! How!

PORTUGUESE: Au! Au!

RUSSIAN: Gav! Gav!

SPANISH: Gau! Gau!

SPANISH (PERU): Gua! Gua! Gua!

SWEDISH: Vov! Vov!

TAGALOG: Ow! Ow!

HIGH TECH HELP

Most experienced dog owners require little help in decoding the utterances of their canine significant other, but those who want computer-coded verification can purchase the Bowlingual Pet Translator, a device developed by the Takara Company, one of Japan's largest toymakers. The Bowlingual is a small wireless microphone that attaches to the dog's collar and transmits the dog's barks to a breed-specific database programmed with over 200 translation patterns. It can tell you if the dog is happy, sad, wary, assertive, frustrated, or needy. The Bowlingual was developed in partnership with a veterinarian and animal behaviorist, and can even be set to a remote diary mode, so that overprotective dog owners—or perhaps those concerned about the fate of their furniture—can get remote readouts of their dog's emotional state while they are away at work.

PUREBRED OR MUTT?

Most "purebred" dog breeds were created from 1850–1930. Prior to that, there were types of dog that fell into rough categories, mostly according to the kind of work they did, but interbreeding was freely practiced among individuals and types with an eye to function rather than "pure breed." Formal "Purebred" registries did not exist prior to the late nineteenth century; the first was the Kennel Club of Great Britain, founded in 1873.

THE MOST ANCIENT
BREEDS OF DOG

According to a study in the journal *Science,* there are 15 breeds of dog that are the most ancient and are the closest genetically to wolves. While some of the dogs in the list, such as the Siberian husky and Alaskan malamute, are no surprise, others that make the almost-wolf grade, such as the Pekingese and Shih tzu, might cause you to be a bit startled and to reconsider before you fasten that rhinestone collar on your lap dog. The list, with the area of origin:

Afghan hound (Afghanistan)
Akita (Japan)
Alaskan malamute (Alaska)
basenji (Congo)
Canaan dog (Israel)
chow chow (China)
Lhasa apso (Tibet)
Pekingese (China)

saluki (Persia)
Samoyed (Siberia)
shar-pei (China)
Shiba Inu (Japan)
Shih tzu (Tibet)
Siberian husky (Siberia)
Tibetan terrier (Tibet)

THE 10 LEAST POPULAR AKC-REGISTERED BREEDS AS OF 2018 WERE: Cirnechi dell'Etna (183rd place); Finnish Spitz (184th place); Cesky Terriers (185th place); American Foxhounds (186th place); Bergamasco Sheepdogs (187th place); English Foxhounds (188th place); Harriers (189th place); Chinooks (190th place); Norwegian Lundehunds (191st place); Sloughis (192nd place).

WORLD'S TOP TEN DOG BREEDS

UNITED STATES

LABRADOR RETRIEVER

GERMAN SHEPHERD

GOLDEN RETRIEVER

FRENCH BULLDOG

BULLDOG

BEAGLE

POODLE

ROTTWEILER

GERMAN SHORTHAIRED POINTER

YORKSHIRE TERRIER

GREAT BRITAIN

LABRADOR RETRIEVER

FRENCH BULLDOG

COCKER SPANIEL

BULLDOG

SPRINGER SPANIEL

GOLDEN RETRIEVER

MINIATURE SMOOTH HAIRED DACHSHUND

PUG

GERMAN SHEPHERD

MINIATURE SCHNAUZER

GERMANY

FRENCH BULLDOG

LABRADOR

AUSTRALIAN SHEPHERD

CHIHUAHUA

GOLDEN RETRIEVER

BORDER COLLIE

LABRADOODLE

RHODESIAN RIDGEBACK

PUG

ROTTWEILER

FRANCE

AUSTRALIAN SHEPHERD

BELGIAN SHEPHERD

STAFFORDSHIRE BULL TERRIER

GOLDEN RETRIEVER

GERMAN SHEPHERD

AMERICAN STAFFORDSHIRE TERRIER

LABRADOR

FRENCH BULLDOG

CAVALIER KING CHARLES SPANIEL

CHIHUAHUA

OODLES ON POODLES

Poodles were developed in Germany in the sixteenth and seventeenth century as water retrievers, but poodle-type dogs have been known in Europe since Roman times. Known as "lion dogs" to the Romans because of their manes, they appear on tombs and Greek and Roman coins. The poodle is a "pan-European" continental dog, more closely associated with France and Germany than with Great Britain. Their name is derived from the German *pudeln,* which means to "splash"; most historical accounts of the poodle state that they are strong swimmers and excellent retrievers.

In France, the breed has always been beloved and the poodle is the French national dog. Historical references to the poodle in France often refer to it as a *Caniche*, derived from *canard*, or "duck," because the poodle was used as a duck dog and retriever. *Barbets* were miniature caniches.

The poodle haircut, which has subjected the breed to so many sniggers over the years, is said to have had a practical origin. Poodle hair does not shed and it grows continuously. If not cut or groomed, it will form dreadlocks, or "cords," like those of a Komondor. In fact, it is permissible to show a corded poodle in AKC shows, although that is rare today. However, the intense coats drag the dog down in the water, accumulate debris, and take a long time to dry, so the custom became to shave the hindquarters to free the dog's limbs for swimming and the muzzle so that it could easily retrieve, but to leave hair around the chest and joints to insulate vital organs in the cold water. The topknots were tied up so the dog could see, and hunters used different color strings or ribbons so that they could distinguish their own dog at a distance in the water. Fast forward to today—and the style is for barrettes and perky little jeweled bows!

POODLE TRICKS

Poodles are highly intelligent and agile and have a whimsical nature that allows them to enjoy performing and quickly learn tricks. There are many accounts of performing poodle acts, as well as less formal "performances," such as the shoeblack in nineteenth-century Paris who conducted his trade near the Pont Neuf. His poodle was trained to notice the shiny boots of passersby, and after rolling in the mud, the dog would muddy the boots of the well-groomed man. Lo and behold, a few yards beyond lurked his master, the shoeblack, ready for business!

Chanda-Leah, a champagne colored toy poodle, held the *Guinness Book of World Records* title for the dog that could perform the most tricks. She had 86 documented tricks, including putting away her toys, untying knots, and fetching tissues if you sneezed.

POODLE FACTOIDS

Something about the intelligence, canniness, and over-the-top hairdos of poodles makes them susceptible to severe spoiling if they get into the wrong human hands:

Aunt March in *Little Women* owned an "awful" poodle.

Gertrude Stein and Alice B. Toklas owned a succession of white standard poodles, Baskets I, II, and III. Most recollections of the Baskets by other writers refer to them as "awful."

On *The Beverly Hillbillies*, Mrs. Drysdale owned Claude, a poodle who was severely discouraged from associating with the Clampett hounds.

Rhapsody In White was the standard poodle shown by the cutthroat professional handler in Christopher Guest's *Best In Show*.

SOME OTHER BREEDS

BLOODHOUND: A breed with a short lifespan, the bloodhound lives an average of only 6¾ years. Sadly, the dog is subject to bloat, or gastric dilatation volvulus, an acute condition when gas builds up in the stomach and causes the stomach to twist on its axis. (The bloodhound is the only dog whose discoveries are accepted as evidence in the courts of law.)

BOYKIN SPANIEL: Hunters developed this breed in the early twentieth century to hunt ducks and turkeys in the swamps of South Carolina. The hunters wanted a dog smaller than the typical retriever, so that it would fit easily into a small hunting boat used in the swamps, and the Boykin is known as "the dog that doesn't rock the boat." The progenitor of the Boykin spaniel is said to be a small stray spaniel-type dog who followed a South Carolina banker as he walked home from church. The banker discovered that the dog had plenty of natural hunting ability and thus gave him to a friend and passionate hunter, Whit Boykin, who developed the breed. Boykins weigh from 25 to 40 pounds (11 to 18 kg) and have a dark brown or liver, curly, waterproof coat. The Chesapeake Bay retriever, springer and cocker spaniels, and American water spaniel were used to develop the Boykin breed.

COLLIE: The breed takes its name from the Scottish black-faced sheep that it guarded, which were known as collies. Early collies were smaller dogs with blunter muzzles than the purebred rough- and smooth-coat collies bred today. Crossbreeding to borzois (Russian wolfhounds) added the height and long noses seen in today's showdog specimens.

After Queen Victoria started keeping collies at Balmoral Castle in Scotland, the breed became fashionable among the elite. J. Pierpont Morgan was an influential collie breeder. In 1906, his Ormskirk Olympian took best of breed at Westminster. Collies may be either smooth- or rough-coated; the smooth-coat type was more often used as a drover's dog to bring stock to market, and the rough-coat type was more commonly used in the fields to herd the sheep.

WHAT A DANDIE!

"He evolved from the Scottish hillside, the gray mists forming his body, a bunch of lichen his topknot, crooked juniper stems his forelegs, and a wet bramble his nose." Thus does Sir Walter Scott describe the type of terrier kept by the farmer Dandie Dinmont in Scott's novel *Guy Mannering* (1875). Dandie Dinmont liked to stick with tradition in his choice of dog names; his six terriers were known as Auld Pepper, Auld Mustard, Young Pepper, Young Mustard, Little Pepper, and Little Mustard! Today, the low-to-the-ground, long-bodied terriers with big heads, houndlike ears, rough coats, and silky, somewhat wild in appearance topknots are known as Dandie Dinmonts after the character in the novel. In 2007, Hobergay's Fineus Fog (Harry), a top-winning Dandie Dinmont belonging to the comedian Bill Cosby, was a favorite to take Best In Show at the Westminster dog show at Madison Square Garden. Harry ended as runner-up to Best In Show winner Champion Felicity's Diamond Jim, a springer spaniel; however,

he had taken 57 previous Best In Shows. The Dandie Dinmont is a relatively uncommon breed; Harry was the only Dandie Dinmont to show at Westminster in 2007. Cosby has owned a large number of show dogs; however, he has yet to name one after Frufy, the dog in his early stand-up comedy routine.

SOME OTHER BREEDS
CONTINUED

MASTIFF: This huge dog is descended from ancient dog breed types known as the Alaunt and the Molosser. It was used as a war dog, guard, and for bear, bull, and lion baiting. (Today, the mastiff is known for its gentle temperament.) Marco Polo wrote that Kublai Khan, the ancient emperor and grandson of Genghis Khan, kept a kennel with 5,000 mastiffs for hunting and as war dogs. Hannibal, the Roman warrior, took battalions of war-trained mastiffs with him when he crossed the Alps. The Saint Bernard, once known as the Alpine mastiff, is said to be the descendant of Hannibal's mastiffs interbred with local Alpine dogs. In the Middle Ages, mastiffs were kept chained during the day and then were released at night to prowl castle grounds as a potent deterrent to intruders. Mastiffs are mentioned in England's first written laws, the Forest Laws of King Canute, which state that the dogs must have their middle toes amputated so that they

will be unable to chase the King's deer. The Legh family of Lyme Hall, Cheshire, have been famous mastiff breeders for generations. King James I, Mary Queen of Scots' son, gave two Lyme Hall mastiffs to Philip II of Spain; these dogs appear in later portraits of the Spanish royal children. Mastiffs were later known as butcher's dogs, presumably because it took a butcher to have access to enough meat to feed them. Famous mastiff owners include King Henry VIII, Emily Brontë (one of the few personal effects we have of Emily Brontë's is her sketch of Keeper, her beloved mastiff), Marlon Brando, Bob Dylan, and Kirstie Alley.

RHODESIAN RIDGEBACK: This dog is a large, shorthaired, golden-wheat colored hunting dog. It's named for a fan-shaped area of hair that forms a ridge by growing in the opposite direction from the rest of the coat; it tapers from immediately behind the shoulder down to the level of the hips. The ridge is the result of a genetic mutation.

SCHIPPERKE: In Flemish, the name of this dog means "Little Captain." Schipperkes are small black dogs who served as barge dogs in Belgium, guarding the barges, killing rats, and "encouraging" the horses who towed the barges.

SHAR-PEI: Its wrinkled skin is a notable feature of the shar-pei. It can have either a "horse coat" (short) or "bear coat" (a longer coat similar to a chow's). "Shar-pei" means "sand skin" or "shark skin," and, in fact, the coat of the shar-pei is prickly and can cause a burning sensation to susceptible humans when they stroke the dog. The shar-pei's wrinkles are caused by a substance, mucin, produced by fibroblasts in their skin. Mucin is said to act like a glue for shar-peis wounded during dogfights; however, the shar-pei can develop a condition called cutaneous mucinosis that causes the mucin to form oozing blisters.

BLACK AND BLUE

The shar-pei and the chow chow are the only blue/black-tongued dog breeds. In China, where both breeds originated, the black tongue was said to be a potent aid to help a barking guard dog protect its family from evil spirits. Chows are born with pink tongues that turn blue-black over the next eight to ten weeks. However, many breeds have tongues that sport blue-black spots over pink! This phenomenon has been documented in over 30 breeds; the spots are simply extra pigment, similar to human freckles.

The chow chow

WILD DOGS

The dingo, which is also called the warrigal or the *Canis lupus* dingo, is a wild dog common to southeast Asia, and is particularly common in Australia. Dingoes were introduced to Australia by aboriginal sea travelers about 3,500 years ago, before the establishment of domesticated canines on the continent, and thus dingoes are considered direct descendants of the early ancestors of modern dogs. Dingoes are medium-size (weighing 20–40 pound/9–18 kg), shorthaired dogs, usually of sandy or earthen color, with erect ears. They have larger canine teeth than domestic dogs and have wrists that rotate, allowing them to use their paws in a handlike manner. Dingoes can climb trees, and they are opportunistic carnivores, eating plants as well as meat. They breed only once a year, and dominant females often kill the pups of lower-ranking females. In Australia, dingoes have interbred extensively with domestic dogs, and as many as one-third of Australian dingoes are now thought to be hybrids. Like many wild canines, they seldom bark.

PARIAH DOGS

"Pariah dogs" is a term that was first applied to the wild dogs of India, but it has been generalized to refer to any of the feral dogs who live and scavenge on the edges of human settlements throughout the world—in the presence of humans but without direct human interaction.

Most pariah dogs have a similar appearance, known as the "long-term pariah morphotype," with yellowish or earth colored, short, thick coats, wedge-shaped heads, and upright ears. Dogs falling into the pariah category include the Korean Jindo, the Aso from the Philippines, the Khoi (Hottentot) from South Africa, Santal hound from India, the Carolina dog, and the New Guinea singing dog. The Carolina dog is a type of wild dog discovered in the 1970s, living in the isolated cypress swamps of the U.S. Southeast.

"SINGING" DOGS

The New Guinea singing dog is native to New Guinea, and because it has been isolated from other dogs on that island for so long, it is thought to be one of the oldest pariah dog types. New Guinea singing dogs howl like wolves, but with a peculiar undulant pitch that has earned them their name.

Another pariah-type dog with unusual vocalizations is the dhole, or Asiatic wild dog, which has been a distinct species within the canid family for thousands of years. Dholes have evolved a unique range of vocalizations, including screams, mews, chatters, clucks, and a sonorous whistle. Basenjis, a registered dog breed that originated in Africa and has a pariah dog-type phenotype, also do not bark. They make a sound called a "barooo"—and that's what it sounds like!

WINNER'S CIRCLE

The first formally organized dog show was held in the Town Hall, Newcastle on Tyne, England, in June 1859. The entry comprised 60 pointers and setters. Since then, dog shows have become a way of life for enthusiasts.

Pointer *Setter*

WESTMINSTER DOG SHOW FACTS

🐾 The first Westminster dog show, which showcased over 1,200 dogs, was held in May 1877 at Gilmore's Gardens (the Hippodrome) in Manhattan. Today, that same site is occupied by the New York Life Building, which houses the offices of the American Kennel Club (AKC), the premier registry for purebred dogs in the United States.

🐾 Westminster began in 1876, when a group of "sporting gentlemen" met regularly in the bar of a Manhattan hotel to tell hunting yarns and brag about their dogs. They named their "club" after their favorite hotel. In the early days, the club kept its own kennel of field trial pointers, and to this day the logo of the Westminster dog show is an English pointer.

🐾 Terriers have won the most Best In Shows (BIS): 48. Fox terriers have won 15 BIS; Scottish terriers have won 8; English springer spaniels (sporting group) 6; 5 BIS for standard poodles; 4 BIS each for Airedale terriers, boxers, Doberman pinschers, smooth fox terriers, American cocker spaniels, Pekingese, and Sealyham terriers.

🐾 In 1909, Ch. Warren Remedy, a smooth fox terrier, won Best In Show for three consecutive years; that has never happened since.

🐾 Entry requirements in the early days were evidently more freewheeling than they are today. The first catalog included a number of intriguing entries, including a dog described as a cross between a Russian setter and a Saint Bernard, and "Nellie . . . born with two legs only." The first show also included two staghounds from the late General George Custer's pack, and two deerhounds bred by Queen Victoria. In 1889, the Czar of Russia exhibited a borzoi, which was listed in the catalog as a "Siberian wolfhound."

SCRUFFTS

Great Britain's Kennel Club (est. 1873) and the American Kennel Club (est. 1884) were both founded to promote and regulate the breeding and showing of purebred dogs. The AKC still specializes in purebred dogs, but the Kennel Club has expanded its stated mission to ". . . promote responsible dog ownership and in every way, the general improvement of dogs." To this generous end, the Kennel Club sponsors not only Crufts, the largest purebred dog show in the world, but Scruffts, a dog show for the mutt (or as the Kennel Club notes with solemn political correctness, ". . . a dog of mixed blood, whose parents are of two different breeds, or a mixture of several breeds." The Kennel Club has registered crossbreds for over 50 years; registered crossbreds can compete in Kennel Club-sponsored obedience, working dog, and agility trials. The AKC restricts participation in these events to purebreds.

Preliminary competitions for Scruffts are run at venues all over Great Britain, building up to the final face-off among the top crossbreeds at the "Discover Dogs" event, held in London each November. Classes include Prettiest Crossbred Bitch, Most Handsome Crossbred Dog, Golden Oldies, and Child's Best Friend (entries in this class are handled by children). The 2006 top Scruffts winner was Dylan, a stray dog rescued from the streets.

WINNER'S CIRCLE
CONTINUED

BEYOND WESTMINSTER

The American Kennel Club, in combination with Eukanuba dog foods (owned by Procter & Gamble) is trying to jazz up the old-fashioned dog show for the twenty-first century with superstars, cash, and television fame. To be eligible to show at Westminster, all that is required of a dog is that it be a dog show champion. However, entry to the AKC/Eukanuba Championship is by invitation only, limited to the year's top winning dogs in each breed, National Specialty Best of Breed winners, and invited top winning competitors from other countries. Significant prize money is offered (the traditional dog show offers little if any prize money): the Best In Show winner of the AKC/Eukanuba Championship wins $50,000 and the breeder of the Best In Show winner gets $15,000. Animal Planet broadcasts the show, and viewers vote for their favorite dog (results announced at the show). The show also serves as a qualifier for Crufts, the largest dog show in the world (see page 29). Along with the conformation competitions, the AKC holds national agility and obedience invitationals. Dog shows used to be relatively low key, but not any more!

THE WORLD'S UGLIEST DOG

This competition is held every year at California's Sonoma-Marin County Fair. Without a doubt, dogs of the Chinese crested breed are the canines to beat at this competition. Sam, a Chinese crested, is a three time repeat World's Ugliest Dog. A bald, warty dog with a few long, scraggly hairs scattered on the top of his head, protruding teeth, and white eyes (due to cataracts), Sam is said to bear a close resemblance to Yoda in the *Star Wars* movies. Sam's girlfriend, Tater Tot, a Chinese crested–Chihuahua mix, is also a serious contender for world's ugliest dog; she has taken world's ugliest mixed breed but never quite ascended to the ne plus ultra of completely ugliest dog. Another Chinese crested contestant, Archie, was adopted by a shelter worker who says that the shelter paid her $10 to take Archie.

TOP DOGS OF THE TOP DOG SHOWS:
BEST IN SHOW WINNERS

YEAR	WESTMINSTER	CRUFTS	AKC/EUKANUBA INVITATIONAL
2013	GCH Banana Joe V Tani Kazari *Affenpinscher*	Soletrader Peek A Boo *Petit basset griffon vendéen*	GCH CH Claircreek Impression De Matisse *Portuguese water dog*
2014	GCH Afterall Painting The Sky *Wire fox terrier*	Afterglow Maverick Sabre *Poodle*	GCH CH Cragsmoor Good Time Charlie *Skye terrier*
2015	GCH Tashtins Lookin For Trouble *Beagle*	McVan's To Russia With Love *Scottish terrier*	GCH CH Lockenhaus' Rumor Has It V Kenlyn *German shepherd*
2016	GCH Vjk-Myst Garbonita's California Journey *Shorthaired pointer*	Burneze Geordie Girl *West Highland white terrier*	GCHB CH Cordmaker Mister Blue Sky *Puli*
2017	GCH Lockenhaus' Rumor Has It V Kenlyn *German shepherd*	Afterglow Miami Ink *American cocker spaniel*	GCHP CH Silverhall Strike Force *Cocker spaniel*
2018	GCH Belle Creek's All I Care About Is Love *Bichon frise*	Collooney Tartan Tease *Whippet*	GCHP CH Pinnacle Tennessee Whiskey *Whippet*
2019	GCH Kingarthur Van Foliny Home *Wire fox terrier*	Planet Waves Forever Young Daydream Believers *Papillon*	GCH CH Pequest Wasabi *Pekingese*

CHAPTER 2

Dogs of the Famous and Rich

Dogs have been man's companion throughout history,

and many relationships of the rich and famous with their

special friends have been recorded. From yesterday's kings

and queens to today's presidents, from writers and artists

of classic works to contemporary celebrities, canines have

been part of the lives of many movers and shakers.

FAMOUS DOGS AND
THEIR PEOPLE

OWNER	OCCUPATION	PET
Jennifer Aniston	American actress	Norman, a corgi-terrier mix
Victoria Beckham	Fashion designer	Fig, an English cocker spaniel
Humphrey Bogart	American actor	Zero, a mongrel
Charles Dickens	British writer	Turk, a mastiff
Sigmund Freud	Austrian psychiatrist	Jo-Fi, a chow chow
Selena Gomez	American singer	Daisy and Winnie, Poodle mixes
Jake Gyllenhaal	American actor	Atticus, a German Shepherd, and Boo Radley, a Puggle
Dakota Johnson	American Actress	Zeppelin, a terrier mix
Stephen King	American writer	Marlow, a Pembroke Welsh corgi
Thomas Hardy	British writer	Wessex, a hairy mongrel
Audrey Hepburn	Dutch-born actress	Mr. Famous, a Yorkshire terrier
Sir Isaac Newton	British scientist	Diamond
Mary Kay Olsen	American actress	Luka, a chocolate Labrador
Joan Rivers	American comedian	Spike, a Yorkshire terrier
Amanda Seyfried	American actress	Finn, Australian shepherd
Shirley Temple	American movie actress	Ching Ching II, a Pekingese
James Thurber	American humorist	Rex, a bull terrier
Justin Timberlake	American musician	Bella and Bearlie, Yorkshire terriers
Rudolph Valentino	Italian actor	Centaur Pendragon, an Irish wolfhound
Reese Witherspoon	American actress and producer	Hank, a chocolate Lab and Pepper, a French bulldog

CELEBRITY TALES

A SHINING STAR

While shooting the movie *True Crime* in Los Angeles, Alicia Silverstone discovered a stray mutt, who was injured and bleeding. The actress gave the dog a home, and Samson, as he was named, even appeared in the hit movie *Clueless*. At last count, Alicia has adopted five dogs, all of them strays. Her acts of kindness don't stop there. The actress is the spokesperson for PETA (People for the Ethical Treatment of Animals) and she has opened an animal shelter on her estate.

HAPPY COUPLES

In 2003, Sigourney Weaver organized the nuptials of her Italian greyhound Petals and a neighbor's Italian greyhound, Jimmy. Weaver retains custody of one of the puppies of the union, Baci ("kisses" in Italian).

When the famous British singer Elton John tied the knot with his partner David Furnish in a civil ceremony, Elton's parti-color (black-and-white) cocker spaniel, Arthur, served as best man at their ceremony.

Oprah once wrote that when her partner Stedman Graham called her when away on business trips, the first thing he always said was "How are the kids?" (meaning their cocker spaniels Solomon and Sophie) and Oprah would think, "Oh no, we've become one of those couples." Oprah's current dogs are two springer spaniels, Sunny and Lauren, and a cocker spaniel named Sadie.

LITERARY DOG LOVERS

Sir Walter Scott (1771–1832), the famous Scottish novelist, kept over 30 dogs during his life, including Douglas and Percy, greyhounds, Camp, a bull terrier, and Maida, his favorite Scottish deerhound. Scott kept the window of his writing studio open in all weathers so that Douglas and Percy could leap in and out at will. The Sir Walter Scott monument in Edinburgh features a marble statue of Sir Walter sitting in a chair with Maida at his feet.

Beneath this sculptured form which late you wore
Sleep soundly, Maida, at your master's door.
THE EPITAPH SCOTT WROTE FOR MAIDA'S TOMB

The country vet Alf Wight (1916–95) used the pen name James Herriot and was author of the best-selling *All Creatures Great and Small* (and several equally popular sequels.) He had many canine companions:

Don (childhood Irish setter)	Hector (Jack Russell terrier)
Dinah and Sam (beagles)	Polly (yellow Labrador)
Dan (black Labrador)	Bodie (border terrier)

The English novelist and essayist Virginia Woolf (1882–1941) was a life-long animal lover whose childhood pets included a squirrel and a mouse. Her first published essay was an obituary to her family's pet dog. Eventually, she wrote the novel *Flush: A Biography*, imagining the life of the poet Elizabeth Barrett Browning's (1806–61) beloved dog—the dog was mentioned in many of Browning's letters to her friends.

The Nobel Prize winning playwright Eugene O'Neill (1888–1953) is not known as an author of simple sentiments, but in "The Last Will and Testament of Silverdene Emblem O'Neill," written in 1940 in the voice of his elderly dalmatian Blemie, O'Neill shows his soft side. Blemie was the beloved companion of O'Neill and his third wife, Carlotta Monterey, during the years they spent at Tao House, in Danville, California. In the will, Blemie tells his master and mistress that dogs do not fear death, counsels them to get another dog (a dalmatian), and bequeathes to his successor his collar and leash, and his overcoat and raincoat, which he notes were made to order in 1929 at Hermès in Paris. Blemie's final words, "Whenever you visit my grave, say to yourselves . . . Here lies one who loves us and whom we loved."

E. B. White (1899–1985), *The New Yorker* writer and *Charlotte's Web* (1952) author, often wrote of his dachshunds Fred and Minnie.

The American author Edith Wharton (1862–1937) often worked in her home in the Berkshires in Massachusetts. In the mornings, she would surround herself with her lapdogs, especially her Pekingese, as she wrote in her bedroom. *Ethan Frome* (1911), one of her more popular novels, was written in this way.

Keeper, a mastiff mix, was just one of the dogs that belonged to the Brontë family. Insights about this intimidating dog appear in Emily Brontë's (1818–48) famous novel *Wuthering Heights* (1847), where the guard dogs have such names as Thrasher, Wolf, and Growler. Her sister Charlotte, also a noted novelist, has written letters in which she mentions Emily wandering the moors with Keeper.

THE DOG ATE MY MANUSCRIPT

The 120-foot (36.5-m) long scroll that is the original manuscript of *On the Road*, Jack Kerouac's famous beat novel, has a chewed edge at the end. There's a hand notation by Kerouac: "Ate by Patchkee, a dog." Patchkee was the cocker spaniel of Lucien Carr, Jack's friend who is famous for having stabbed David Kammerer, who was obssessed with Carr, to death in 1944.

A TERRIER IN THE WHITE HOUSE

Throughout American history, many different pets have lived in the White House, some becoming famous in their own right.

Although the First Pets have differed greatly in species, from John Quincy Adams' alligator and silkworms to Benjamin Harrison's goat and opposums, dogs have been the most popular presidential pet. A few have even acquired their own small share of fame, such as Him and Her, Lyndon B. Johnson's beagles, which made the cover of *Life* magazine in June 19, 1964, and Millie, Barbara Bush's springer spaniel. The former First Lady wrote a book about the White House seen through Millie's eyes, which topped *The New York Times* bestseller list for more than 20 weeks. Eight presidents have owned terriers, making them the most popular presidential dogs.

PRESIDENT	DOG'S NAME	BREED
Theodore Roosevelt	Blackjack	Manchester terrier
	Pete	Bull terrier
	Skip	Rat terrier
Woodrow Wilson	Bruce	Bull terrier
Herbert Hoover	Big Ben	Fox terrier
	Sonnie	Fox terrier
Franklin D. Roosevelt	Fala	Scottish terrier
	Meggie	Scottish terrier
John F. Kennedy	Charlie	Welsh terrier
Richard Nixon	Pasha	Yorkshire terrier
George W. Bush	Barney	Scottish terrier
	Miss Beazley	Scottish terrier
Barack Obama	Bo	Portuguese water dog
	Sunny	Portuguese water dog
Joe Biden	Champ	German shepherd
	Major	German shepherd

PRESIDENTIAL PACK

George Washington kept a foxhound pack; the hounds were named Drunkard, Mopsey, Taster, Cloe, Tipsy, Tipler, Forester, Captain, Lady Rover, Vulcan, Sweet Lips, and Searcher. For some reason, Washington seems to have relied heavily on an alcoholic motif in his choice of names.

FDR AND FALA

Although most presidents have had dogs, one sometimes gets the feeling that the dog is mostly trotted out for photo ops and otherwise is spending a lot of time in the White House kennel on a daily basis. That was not the case with FDR's Scottish terrier, Fala (1940–52). FDR and Fala were inseparable, and even today, a statue of Fala sits at the knee of the president's statue at the FDR Memorial in Washington. Fala is buried next to the president in the rose garden at FDR's Hyde Park, New York, home, the only presidential dog accorded such an honor. Fala was given to FDR as a puppy by Daisy Suckley, FDR's cousin. FDR fed the dog by hand every day and Fala traveled everywhere with the president and slept at the foot of Roosevelt's bed. In 1944, FDR used Fala as the theme of a speech to make fun of Republicans who had complained that FDR had sent a Navy destroyer to retrieve Fala when he was inadvertently left behind on the Aleutian Islands—which was untrue. Roosevelt noted that as a true Scotsman, Fala did not take kindly to personal attacks.

Fala was only five when FDR died of a cerebral hemorrhage. Fala attended the funeral and then was briefly sent back to Daisy Suckley, but the president's wife, Eleanor, missed Fala and asked for him back. Until his death at the age of 12, Fala and Fala's grandson, Tomas, kept Eleanor company at Hyde Park. Eleanor wrote that Fala never stopped watching for FDR. Fala's leather collar (with a silver plate engraved "Fala, The White House"), braided leather leash, Navajo blanket, and wool coat are on display at the FDR presidential museum.

DESIGNER DOG HOUSE

Lyndon Johnson designed a doghouse for his beagles, Him and Her, which featured floodlights, heat, and Dutch doors. The latter was presumably so that Johnson could hoist the dogs up by the ears (a habit of his) without having to first set them loose, which would give them the opportunity to escape his attentions!

REGAL CANINES

U rian was the greyhound of
Anne Boleyn, Henry the VIII's
unfortunately beheaded second queen.
The word "Urian" referred to a devil's
helper or foul fiend; Boleyn's choice of name
for her pet helped to spread the rumor that
she practiced witchcraft, a serious charge in
Tudor times. Some stories say that Urian was
an Italian greyhound; however, Henry VIII's
accounts for September 1530 note that
10 shillings was paid out by the King for a

cow killed by Urian—this implies that Urian was a full-sized greyhound. Legend
has it that Urian accompanied his mistress to the block, but was himself spared
her terrible fate.

> *All I observed was the silliness of the King,*
> *playing with his dogs all the while*
> *and not minding the business.*
> SAMUEL PEPYS, *DIARY*, SEPTEMBER, 1666

Queen Elizabeth II has owned more than 30 Pembroke Welsh corgis
during her reign, starting with Susan, who was a present to her for her eighteenth
birthday in 1944. The queen's father, King George VI, was the first royal to
bring home a corgi. History has not recorded whether he asked, "Can I keep him,
please, huh?" Many of the Queen's subsequent corgis have been descendants
of Susan. Queen Elizabeth II currently has five corgis: Emma, Linnet, Monty,
Holly, and Willow. A royal tragedy occurred when one of the Queen's favorite
older dogs, Pharos, was attacked and killed by Florence (not Dotty, as initially
reported), a bull terrier belonging to the queen's daughter, Princess Anne.

The Queen is also fond of a hybrid known as the "dorgi." The first royal dorgi was the result of a mating between one of the Queen's corgis with a dachshund named Pipkin, who belonged to the Queen's sister, Princess Margaret. The Queen currently has two dorgis: Candy and Vulcan. As well as corgis and dorgis, the Queen also breeds and trains Labradors and cocker spaniels at Sandringham. There is a special Sandringham strain of black Labrador founded in 1911.

LET THEM EAT PUPPY CHOW

Marie Antoinette (1755–93), the unfortunate eighteenth-century French queen, was treated traitorously by humans throughout her life, so it is little wonder that she clung to her dogs for comfort. She is said to have gone to the guillotine clutching one of her tiny dogs, Thisbe, who was most likely a papillon. (Some say Thisbe was a spaniel; however, the papillon was also known as a squirrel spaniel in early days, due to its tail, which is carried curled over its back like that of a squirrel.) Papillons were a highly popular breed at the French court—Madame de Pompadour, the famed courtesan, owned two papillons named Inez and Mimi.

Born Maria Antonia in Austria, Marie Antoinette was renamed when her mother, Empress Maria Theresa of Austria, sent her off to France to marry the 17-year-old Dauphin Louis (King Louis XVI from 1774). The French were anxious to strip Maria/Marie of her Austrian roots and turn her into a creature of the French; the child Maria was forced to leave even her Austrian dog behind her at the border, along with her name. The French were highly critical of their new imported queen and referred to her as *L'Autrichienne*, or the Austrian dog.

Marie Antoinette tried to console herself with luxuries. For her dogs, she created tiny palaces within palaces; at her famous "playhouse," Le Petit Trianon, there are ornate little indoor houses for dogs, some lined with turquoise silk. These have inspired many luxurious twenty-first century imitations, including "Precious Palaces," a line of individually handcrafted interior dog houses designed by New York City designer Betsy Boggs.

CHAPTER 3

Fictional Dogs

The tender feelings that dog lovers have for their canine

companions have not gone unrecorded—poets, novelists

and memoirists, filmmakers, and artists have all used their

talents to express their devotion to their canine partners.

Perhaps it's because the dogs in our lives make us so happy

that they are a popular subject—and then there is the

poignancy of their too short lives.

DOG WRITERS WHO LEAD
THE PACK

THE WOLF WITHIN

Jack London (1876–1916) wrote about dogs with particular emphasis on the struggle for survival in a harsh world. London identified with this struggle—abandoned by his father and raised in poverty, he was self-educated and worked as a seaman, coal shoveler, and gold prospector before finding success as a writer. He writes of canines that are usually part wolf and that must get in touch with their wolfish natures in order to survive. London's major canine-centered works are *The Son of the Wolf* (1900), *Diable, A Dog* (later retitled *Batard*; 1902), *The Call of the Wild* (1903), *White Fang* (1906), and *Brown Wolf* (in the 1907 short story collection *Love of Life*).

RED RULES

Jim Kjelgaard (1910–59) is best known for his series of novels about a family of Irish setters, *Big Red* (1949), *Irish Red* (1951), and *Outlaw Red* (1953). However, besides the red setter series, Kjelgaard also wrote over 40 novels for young adults, with the majority of books about dogs, a few on horses, and always, on the outdoors, including *Desert Dog* (greyhound), *Double Challenge* (collie), *Stormy* (golden retriever), *Snow Dog* and *Wild Trek* (huskies), and *A Nose for Trouble* (bloodhound). Kjelgaard was born in New York City, but grew up in the Allegheny Mountains of Pennsylvania, where he hunted, fished, and generally lived the outdoor life that is so well portrayed in his novels. Contrary to the contemporary opinion that the Irish setter is a beautiful airhead, the red setters of Kjelgaard's novels are always strong, noble, devoted, intelligent, superb bird dogs, and wise in the ways of the Wintapi woods.

Kjelgaard's daughter, Karen, has stated that although the family did have an Irish setter, a gift from Rudd Weatherwax, Lassie's trainer (see page 65), the real Big Red is actually based on a black crossbred setter that Kjelgaard owned as a child. Big Red was made into a Disney movie in 1962, after Kjelgaard's untimely death. He took his own life at only 49 years old; for many years he had experienced chronic depression, possibly caused by a recurrence of a brain tumor that had first developed when he was a child.

FRIEND OR SLAVE?

Elizabeth Marshall Thomas has written *Certain Poor Shepherds*, a novel that perceives the Nativity story from the perspective of a sheepdog, and *Reindeer Moon*, a novel set in the Paleolithic era that includes a wonderful fictional depiction of early humans and wolves living in close proximity. However, her nonfiction work is probably better known due to her 1993 surprise bestseller, *The Hidden Lives of Dogs*. Thomas is an atypical dog lover and writer. For one thing, she eschews most dog training and is scornful of the culture of the purebred dog—facts that make Thomas anathema to many in the American dog establishment.

Thomas holds dogs in the highest esteem. Her general approach is to live alongside dogs and to observe them (Thomas has a strong background in anthropology) for what they can teach us about our own subverted animal nature. She has commented, "Perhaps our hope of redemption lies in the fact that we are animals, not that we are people." Thomas is also one of the few dog writers who states boldly that our beloved dogs are also our slaves. After all, we breed and sell them at will, they live at our pleasure, we can and do put legions of them to death every day. To Thomas, this fact also means that we have an obligation to try to observe dogs as they want to live, to try to allow dogs to live among their own kind as much as possible, rather than attempting to subdue them to roles in our rather demeaning human culture. *The Social Lives of Dogs: The Grace of Canine Company* (2000) is another of her studies of dogs.

DOG WRITERS WHO
LEAD THE PACK
CONTINUED

COOL COLLIES

Montana native Donald McCaig writes of border collies with the eye of a poet, philosopher, and connoisseur. After a successful career in advertising, in the 1970s he bought a sheep farm in Virginia and became a devotee of the working border collie. McCaig fought to keep the AKC from recognizing the border collie breed, fearing that the working characteristics of the dog would be harmed through overemphasis on appearance. His canine-centered works include *Nop's Trials, Nop's Hope, Eminent Dogs: Dangerous Men* (the saga of his journey through Scotland to find the border collie of his dreams), *The Dog Wars: How The Border Collie Battled the American Kennel Club*, and *A Useful Dog* (a collection of short pieces).

IT'S A MYSTERY

Susan Conant's very enjoyable Holly Winter mystery series provides a realistic picture of a true dog fanatic. Holly Winter, Maine native and resident of Cambridge, Massachusetts, is a columnist for *Dog's Life* magazine who shows her malamutes in obedience and conformation AKC dog shows. Holly's boyfriend is Steve Delaney, her veterinarian. When Holly marries Steve, their combined household has five dogs: malamutes Rowdy, Kimi, and Sammy, the shy pointer Lady, and India, a German shepherd. Holly's father, Buck, a Maine outdoorsman type, raises wolf dogs, but he later marries Gabrielle, who owns a bichon frise! Holly's best friend, Rita, is a Cambridge psychotherapist (and yes, Rita does privately think that Holly could use some counseling about her dog obsession). One of the pleasures of the series is Conant's neat ability to satirize both the dog show and Cambridge therapeutic cultures. In real life, Conant, a Radcliffe graduate, shows Alaskan malamutes and has a PhD in human development.

STORYBOOK DOGS

NAME	BREED	BOOK	AUTHOR
Argos	Not known	*Odyssey*	Homer
Bodger	Bull terrier	*The Incredible Journey*	Sheila Burnford
Buck	Half shepherd, half Saint Bernard	*Call of the Wild*	Jack London
Bullseye	Staffordshire bull terrier	*Oliver Twist*	Charles Dickens
Fluffy	Enormous 3-headed guard dog	*Harry Potter and the Sorcerer's Stone*	J. K. Rowling
Hound of the Baskervilles	(*see below*)*	*The Hound of the Baskervilles*	Sir Arthur Conan Doyle
Jip	Not known	*Doctor Dolittle stories*	Hugh Lofting
Lassie	Collie	*Lassie Come Home/ Lassie's Rescue Rangers*	Eric Knight
Nana	Newfoundland	*Peter Pan*	J. M. Barrie
Pongo	Dalmatian	*The Hundred and One Dalmatians*	Dodie Smith
Precious	Toy poodle	*The Silence of the Lambs*	Thomas Harris
Timmy	Border collie	*The Famous Five* series	Enid Blyton
Toto	Cairn terrier	*The Wizard of Oz*	Frank L. Baum

* It was not a pure bloodhound and not a pure mastiff; but it appeared to be a combination of the two—gaunt, savage, and as large as a small lioness.

TALES OF SOUTHERN HOUNDS

BOOK	BREED	LOCALE	FATE OF THE DOG
Old Yeller by Fred Gipson Honor: 1957 Newbery Medal	"Yaller" dog	Texas Hill country, nineteenth century	Contracts rabies and must be killed
Sounder by William Armstrong Honor: 1970 Newbery Medal	Coonhound-bloodhound mix	Louisiana, 1930s	Previously shot and maimed by a sheriff; the aged dog's body is found dead in the woods, alongside the body of the boy's unfortunate sharecropper father
Where the Red Fern Grows (1961) by Wilson Rawls	Red bone coonhounds (Old Dan and Little Ann)	Ozark Mountains	Old Dan is killed by a mountain lion defending his boy; Little Ann dies of grief, on Old Dan's grave
The Voice of Bugle Ann by MacKinlay Kantor	Foxhound	Missouri	Disappears; her collar is found with her bones; her voice becomes a ghostly presence in the hills
Algonquin, the Story of a Great Dog by Dion Henderson	English pointer	Grand Junction, Tennessee	After a last field trial triumph, the ailing dog is shot in the head by his master's grandfather
Shiloh by Phyllis Reynold Naylor Honor: 1993 Newbery Medal	Beagle	Rural West Virginia	A young boy must decide how to deal with the fact that he knows a beagle puppy is being abused by its hunter owner

WHAT JENNY ATE:
THE COMPLETE MENU

Maurice Sendak's *Higgelty Piggelty Pop!, or There Must Be More to Life* tells the tale of Jenny, a Sealyham terrier who is discontented, despite having "everything" (her own comb and brush, two bottles of pills, eyedrops, eardrops, a thermometer, a red wool sweater for cold weather, two windows to look out of, two bowls to eat from, and a master who loves her). Jenny sets out into the world to discover what more there is to life. Along the way she finds plenty to eat, including:

leaves
tuna on rye
ham, Swiss, and Russian dressing on pumpernickel
anchovy, tomato, and egg on toast
turkey, bacon, and mayonnaise (she picks out the lettuce)
liverwurst and onion on white bread
salami (her favorite)
raspberry yogurt and farmer's cheese
a pint of milk
the insides of a dozen brown eggs
buttermilk pancakes with syrup
coffee
orange juice
soft-boiled egg with the shell, and a mop made of salami.

The real Jenny was Sendak's Sealyham terrier. Sendak said that Jenny was aging when he wrote the book; writing it was a way to feel that she would live on. Sendak, who died in 2012, was devoted to dogs; he lived alone but always kept a dog, most recently German shepherds, including Max, Runge, and Herman. Sendak's *Some Swell Pup, or, Are You Sure You Want a Dog?* was written with dog trainer Matthew Margolis. The book's illustrations show the new puppy peeing and pooping as new puppies do, copiously and inappropriately. When kids stop laughing, they are likely to get the message that puppies are a responsibility.

OTHER DOG TALES

A DOG OF FLANDERS

The original novel was written by Marie Louise de la Ramée, a British-French author. It tells the pathetic tale of Nello, a poverty-stricken orphan boy who lives with his grandfather and his beloved dog Patrasche in a hovel outside Antwerp, Belgium. Patrasche had been rescued by Nello after being almost beaten to death. Nello sells milk to help his grandfather, and Patrasche willingly pulls the cart for him. Nello is also a talented artist and his dream is to see the Rubens paintings in Antwerp Cathedral, but he lacks the coins he must pay to enter the cathedral. Many vicissitudes ensue, and Nello's grandfather dies. On Christmas Eve, Nello and Patrasche find the cathedral open and sneak inside. The next morning, they are found frozen to death in front of the great Rubens painting *The Raising of the Cross*. To this day, this story is a favorite of the Japanese, and six movie versions have been made of the story, in 1914, 1935, 1960, 1975 (Japan), 1992 (Japan), and 1999.

BORIS THE BOARHOUND

In *The Little Princess* (1905), by Frances Hodgson Burnett, the heroine Sara Crewe is given a "splendid Russian boarhound" with a grand gold and silver collar bearing the inscription: "I am Boris; I Serve the Princess Sara."

SOME CHILDREN'S DOG BOOKS

Lad (Alfred Payson Terhune)
The Incredible Journey (Sheila Burnford)
Julie of the Wolves (Jean Craighead George)
Corgiville Fair (Tasha Tudor)
The Plague Dogs (Richard Adams)
Harry the Dirty Dog (Gene Zion)
The Poky Little Puppy (Janette Sebring Lowrey)
Ribsy (Beverly Cleary)
Ginger Pye (Eleanor Estes)
Junket (Anne H. White)

DOGGY ODES

The Song of Quoodle by G. K. Chesterton
His Apologies by Rudyard Kipling
The Twa Dogs by Robert Burns
To Flush My Dog by Elizabeth Barrett Browning
Old Dog Tray by Stephen Foster
Dinah in Heaven by Rudyard Kipling
The Power of the Dog by Rudyard Kipling

SERIAL DOGS

In the 1950s and 1960s, Grosset & Dunlap, the publisher known for juvenile series, such as Nancy Drew and the Hardy Boys, published a dog book series. Some were reissues of classic dog authors, such as Albert Payson Terhune and Jim Kjelgaard; however, lesser known dog classics are well represented. There are over 30 books in the series, most available today from a variety of on-line sources.

THE CANINE OUEVRE OF COLONEL S. P. MEEK— JUVENILE DOG BOOK AUTHOR EXTRAORDINAIRE

The books in this series of juvenile dog books were first published between 1932 and 1956.

Jerry, the Adventures of an Army Dog
Gypsy Lad: The Story of a Champion Setter
Franz: A Dog of the Police
Dignity: A Springer Spaniel
Rusty, A Cocker Spaniel
Gustav, a Son of Franz: A Police Dog in Panama
Pat: The Story of a Seeing Eye Dog
Boots, the Story of a Working Sheep Dog
Ranger, a Dog of the Forest Service

Hans, A Dog of the Border Patrol
Surfman: The Adventures of a Coast Guard Dog
Red, a Trailing Bloodhound
Boy, An Ozark Coon Hound
Rip, a Game Protector
Omar, a State Police Dog
Pierre of the Big Top: the Story of a Circus Poodle
So You're Going to Get a Puppy: A Dog-Lover's Handbook

MORE LITERARY TIDBITS

In Madeleine L'Engle's *A Wrinkle in Time* series, Fortinbras and Ananda are semimagical dogs.

Genevieve is the hound that pulls Madeline from the Seine in Ludwig Bemelman's *Madeline*.

Paul Auster's 2000 novel, *Timbuktu*, is written in the voice of Mr. Bones, the canine companion to New York City street bum Willy Christmas.

The Dialogue of the Dogs is by Miguel de Cervantes, the author of *Don Quixote*. Cervantes gives two dogs voices for a night, and they tell all about their experiences with different masters.

Three Stories You Can Read to Your Dog, (*The Burglar, The Bone,* and *The Wild Dog*), by Sarah Swan Miller, are stories written to be read aloud to dogs.

Dog is My Copilot, by the editors of *The Bark* (a canine magazine), has short pieces by great writers on the world's oldest friendship. Contributors include Anne Patchett, Alice Walker, and Maxine Kumin.

In *Anna Karenina*, Tolstoy writes an entire chapter from the point of view of Laska, Levin's hunting setter

dog. Laska and Levin are hunting snipe, and Laska's thoughts show us how she humors her master, who she finds so sadly deficient in the necessary senses for hunting.

Beem (1978) by Gavril Troyepolsky, translated from the Russian, is the story of a tricolor Gordon setter.

I and Dog is by the Monks of New Skete (the famous monks who breed German shepherds and train dogs in upstate New York). They have also authored the classic *How To be Your Dog's Best Friend* and *How to Raise A Puppy You Can Live With*.

Golden Retrievals is a poem by Mark Doty in his collection *Sweet Machine*.

What The Dog Did: Tales From A Reluctant Dog Owner was written by Emily Yoffe.

Fairy Wogdog appears in *Watership Down*, by Richard Adams. as the Messenger of the great Dog Spirit of the East.

Queen Dripslobber is another canine character in *Watership Down*. He appears in Dandelion's story "Rowsby Woof and the Fairy Wogdog."

COMIC STRIP DOGS

STRIP TITLE	CREATOR	A FEW DETAILS
Dogbert, in *Dilbert* (1989)	Scott Adams	Dilbert's smarter, sardonic alter ego is a dog who works as a management consultant; Dogbert tries to exorcise the demons of stupidity that he sees in the works of man.
Electra and Vivian, in *Cathy* (1976)	Cathy Guisewite	Electra is Cathy's dog; Vivian is Irving's. Both were adopted from shelters; when Irving got Vivian, for a while she became the "only" female in his life, but as a dog person, Cathy understood. In 2005, Electra and Vivian were ringbearers when Cathy and Irving finally got married.
Farley, in *For Better or For Worse* (1979)	Lynne Johnston	Farley, an old English sheepdog, was a regular in this strip; he was 14 years old when he saved April, the Pattersons' youngest daughter, from drowning, but as a result died of a heart attack.
Marmaduke (1954)	Brad Anderson	Marmaduke (a good natured, disaster-prone Great Dane) is smart because he's eaten so much homework!
Otto, in *Beetle Bailey* (1950)	Mort Walker	Otto and Sarge are joined at the hip. They are both portly, buck toothed, big eaters, and BOTH wear sergeant uniforms.
Snoopy in *Peanuts* (1950)	Charles M. Schulz	The beagle, who is Charlie Brown's companion, is known for his daydreams of being a writer and a World War I flying ace.

CARTOON DOGS
OF THE 1960S

Cartoon series first made a real impact on television viewers in the 1960s. Several of the most popular shows were produced by the legendary team of William Hanna and Joseph Barbera, whose first groundbreaking series was *Huckleberry Hound*. Other hits featuring canines followed, including *The Jetsons* and *The Flintstones*. The team had a major influence on other animators.

HUCKLEBERRY HOUND

The series first appeared in 1958 and became a 1960s' classic. Huck was a blue dog in a porkpie hat who spoke in a slow southern drawl, voiced by Daws Butler. The drawl was rumored to be based on the soft North Carolina intonations of film and TV star Andy Griffith. Huck was good natured, unflappable, and fond of droning the traditional old ditty "My Darling Clementine," although his singing voice left much to be desired. Like many a Shakespearean character, Huck was also a master of the explanatory aside, providing cartoon viewers with a running narrative of his motives during his many cartoonish misadventures. In 1960, *Huckleberry Hound* won an Emmy, the first cartoon series to do so.

THE JETSONS

Astro was a stray discovered by Elroy, the Jetson's little boy. George, the futuristic dad, doesn't want to keep Astro—he prefers a trouble-free electronic dog—but Astro saves the day by (accidentally) rescuing George from a burglar. Baby boomers will remember the final scene of each *Jetsons* episode, set to the bouncy, space-happy *Jetsons* theme: George is complacently "walking" Astro on an automatic dog walker suspended in Space outside the Jetson's launchpad home. Astro sees a cat and in no time, cat and Astro are sitting interestedly by while George gets more aerobic exercise than he bargained for on an out-of-control dog walker. Every episode ended with George's scream, "Jane! Stop this crazy thing!!!!!" Astro's signature line, "Ruh Roh (Uh oh!) George!" was voiced by Don Messick.

THE FLINTSTONES

OK, maybe Dino was supposed to be a dinosaur, but his behavior was pure canine. Dino achieved his television immortality in the opening segment of every *Flintstones* episode, when he greeted home-from-work Fred with a hysterically happy "Yiyiyiyiyiyi!" and a full body tackle that had Fred crying for mercy.

MR. PEABODY

Created by Ted Key, the originator of the *Hazel* comic strip, Mr. Peabody was a professorial sort of dog who owned his own (eager and good-natured) boy, Sherman. The scholarly Mr. Peabody wore enormous horn rims that were mimicked by Sherman. Through 91 episodes, Mr. Peabody and Sherman traveled in time in the "Wayback" machine to different historical eras of the past, and, through timely intervention, helped history come out right every time. Each Mr. Peabody episode ended with one of Peabody's awful puns. Mr. Peabody's voice was provided by Bill Scott, the series producer.

UNDERDOG

The voice of Underdog (who always talked in rhyme) was provided by Wally Cox. Polly Purebred, Underdog's girlfriend (the character of *Superman's* Lois Lane as a cocker spaniel), had only to warble, "Oh where, oh where, has my Underdog gone?" to send Underdog (in his alias as Shoeshine Boy) into a phone booth to emerge as the masked and caped Underdog, ready to fight the evil villain Dr. Simon Bar Sinister. "When Polly's in trouble, I am not slow! So it's hip, hip, hip and away I go!" was Underdog's signature line, along with "Have no fear—Underdog is here!" Tam Tam the Chiseler was Underdog's evil twin. In 2007, a live-action movie based on the *Underdog* cartoons was released, starring Jim Belushi.

> *The great pleasure of a dog is that you may make a fool of yourself with him and not only will he not scold you, but he will make a fool of himself, too.*
> SAMUEL BUTLER (1835–1902), BRITISH NOVELIST
> FROM *NOTE-BOOKS*, 1912

MOVIES FEATURING DOGS

 *Rescued By Rover* (1905) was one of the first films of the silent-film era to be shot as one continuous narrative instead of a series of self-contained "acts." Directed by pioneering British director Cecil Hepworth, the film starred his family dog, a collie mix named Blair. The six-minute short, which shows Rover rescuing a baby from Gypsies, was so successful that Hepworth had to remake it twice because the original two negatives wore out. Trading on the success of his canine star, Hepworth shot two more dog star vehicles, *Dumb Sagacity* (1907), starring Rover and a horse, and *The Dog Outwits the Kidnappers* (1908). Hepworth's narrative style was an influence on the early American film pioneer D. W. Griffith.

Brawn of the North (1922) was an early movie made with the German shepherd silent-film star Strongheart (see page 60).

Lassie Come Home (1943) is the original Lassie movie. Based on a short story by Eric Knight, the drama is set in Yorkshire, England, during World War I. The parents of a poor boy, Joe Carraclough (Roddy McDowall), are forced to sell the beloved family collie to the Duke of Rudling. Priscilla, the daughter of the Duke, is played by the young Elizabeth Taylor.

The Hound of the Baskervilles (1939) is based on Arthur Conan Doyle's classic Sherlock Holmes story. This is the movie version featuring Basil Rathbone as Holmes and Nigel Bruce as Watson (the first of their 14 Holmes pairings). A desolate mansion on the Devonshire moors, a gruesome death, and—the legend of a demonic hound! The game is afoot, and Holmes is on the trail.

Lady and the Tramp (1955) is Walt Disney's first full-length animated feature based on an original story—or almost. When a stern aunt with two spoiled cats is left in charge of the family's baby, the miffed cocker spaniel Lady runs away and meets Tramp, a mutt from the wrong side of the tracks. At one point in the tale, after Lady has returned home, a rat threatens the new baby and Tramp rushes to the rescue, only to be accused by mean Aunt Clara of instigating the attack—a plot line obviously based on the story of Guinefort/Gelert (see page 79). The movies songs are sung by Peggy Lee.

Old Yeller (1957), a Disney movie based on the Fred Gipson classic juvenile novel, is a boy's coming of age story set in Texas. Tommy comes to love Old Yeller, the stray "yaller "dog that helps him out on the homestead while Tommy's father is gone on a cattle drive. Defending the family from a rabid wolf, Old Yeller is bitten and Tommy is forced to shoot his own dog (played by Spike, owned and trained by the Weatherwax family of trainers). Dad comes home in time to counsel Tommy, and major lessons ensue.

The Shaggy Dog (1959), Disney's first live-action comedy, was based on Felix Salten's 1923 novel, *The Hound of Florence*, about a man who turns into a dog on alternate days. Disney's version, one of the top grossing films of 1959, stars Fred MacMurray and Mouseketeers Tommy Kirk and Annette Funicello (as Wilby's high school love interest). MacMurray plays an irascible mailman with the traditional occupational loathing of dogs. In a cruel twist of fate, his teenage son, Wilby (Kirk) finds a magic ring cursed by the Borgias and is transfigured into a large Bratislavian sheepdog. This is good news to Wilby's little brother, Moochie, who has always wanted a dog and is pleased that his big brother has obligingly turned into one—but the new canine in the family is a test of MacMurray's paternal instincts. The movie's action is moved along by goofy subplots involving espionage and a Professor Plumcutt, who helps Wilby defuse the Borgia curse.

MORE MOVIES
FEATURING DOGS

Big Red (1962) is based on the Jim Kjelgaard story of a show Irish setter owned by Mr. Haggin, a wealthy outdoorsman, and Danny, a trapper in the Wintapi wilderness who loves (and is loved by) Big Red.

The Incredible Journey (1963). This gripping story features three animals of different ages and abilities, but with a strong familial bond, working together to survive as instinct drives them on a journey across the wilderness of Ontario toward home. The unusual companions are Luath, a young Labrador, Bodger, an old English bull terrier, and Tao, a Siamese cat. The cat and the aging bull terrier have a special friendship, with Luath being the youngest addition to the pack. This is the original film version; the 1993 remake was titled *Homeward Bound: The Incredible Journey*, and there was another sequel, *Homeward Bound: Lost in San Francisco* (1996).

Benji (1974) is the story of a homeless dog adopted by a family with a lot of kids. When the kids are kidnapped, it's Benji to the rescue. The dog's character proved so popular that a canine movie franchise was born:

Benji Takes a Dive at Marineland
Benji at Work
Benji Call Home
Benji in Ghost Town
Benji in Puppy Love
Benji the Hunted
Benji's Very Own Christmas Story
Oh Heavenly Dog
Benji: Off the Leash

The Accidental Tourist (1988) is based on the Anne Tyler novel, featuring William Hurt as Macon Leary, the repressed owner of Edward, an irrepressible Welsh corgi. Geena Davis plays Muriel, dog trainer from the Bow Meow Animal Hospital, who brings both Edward and Macon to heel.

🐾 *Turner & Hooch* (1989) stars Tom Hanks, an extremely neat (in the Felix Unger mold) dog-hating detective called Turner, who is forced to adopt the dog of a murder victim, because the dog—a huge, slobbery mastiff—is the only link to the crime. The dog dies while saving Turner's life. Before this happens, his veterinarian becomes Turner's love interest, and her collie makes Hooch a proud daddy, albeit posthumously. Of course, one of the pups looks just like his dad. Hooch is played by a dogue de Bordeaux, a rare breed of French mastiff.

🐾 *Beethoven* (1992) is the story of a Saint Bernard that is rescued from a dognapping only to wreak havoc on the life of a well-ordered suburban family. Later, the dog only just escapes from an evil veterinarian who does dog experiments; the no longer well-ordered suburban family ends up adopting the whole laboratory of dogs. (Four sequels, plus an animated series, were spun off from the original movie).

🐾 *Shiloh* (1996), based on the Newbery Award-winning novel by Phyllis Reynold Naylor, is about a boy who tries to save a beagle from the dog's owner, an abusive hunter.

🐾 *101 Dalmatians* (1996), Disney's remake of the 1961 animated film *One Hundred and One Dalmatians* (which was based on the novel by Dodie Smith) starred Glenn Close as the evil Cruella de Vil, who steals puppies to make into fur coats. Jeff Daniels starred as Roger, who saved and adopted the dalmatians.

🐾 *Best In Show* (2000) is Christopher Guest's hilarious takeoff on the world of dog shows. Featuring shih tzu owner Stefan Vanderhoof, Rhapsody In White, a poodle owned by Sherri Ann Ward Cabot, and the Flecks—who have maxed out their charge card but are willing to bunk in a hotel storage room so that Winky, their Norwich terrier, can have her shot at dog show immortality.

TINSELTOWN STARS

 JEAN, THE VITAGRAPH DOG

A canine star of the silent-movie era, Jean appeared in many movies made
by her owner, Larry Trimble of the Vitagraph studios in Brooklyn, New York.
Jean was a medium-size, old-style (blunt-nose), tricolor collie. From 1908–13,
Trimble directed many short movies starring Jean, often costarring with the
human silent-movie star Florence Turner. Jean's starring vehicles included
Jean and the Calico Doll, Jean and the Waif, Jean goes Fishing, and *A Sailor's
Sacrifice*. Jean even had a salary—$25 a week, not too bad for a dog in the early
twentieth century. Jean died in 1916, and in 1925, Larry Trimble retired from
movie making and became a guide dog trainer.

 STRONGHEART

A German shepherd originally trained for police work in Germany, Strongheart
(1917–29) was another canine silent-movie star who owed his career to Larry
Trimble, as well as Trimble's wife, Jane Murfin. Strongheart's German given
name was Etzel von Oeringen. He was extremely popular, appearing in *White
Fang* (1925), an adaptation of the Jack London classic, as well as *The Silent Call*
(1921), *Brawn of the North* (1922), *The Love Master* (1924), and *The Return
of Boston Blackie* (1927; this is the only Strongheart movie still surviving today).
In 1954, J. Allen Boone wrote *Kinship With All Life*, one of the earliest books
to discuss human/animal psychic and spiritual communication. Boone was first
inspired by the bond he formed with Strongheart when he cared for the dog
while Trimble was away on business trips. Strongheart's enormous popularity set
the stage for Rin Tin Tin, the next German shepherd star who arrived (via radio
shows) in 1930. Strongheart died from complications of burns that he received
when he fell and was burned by hot studio lights.

 RIN TIN TIN

The original Rin Tin Tin was a week-old puppy discovered by Lee Duncan,
an American soldier in France, just a few months before the end of World War I.
Duncan insisted that his unit search a dog kennel that had been bombed. Inside

the kennel he found a litter of well-bred German shepherd pups. Duncan brought Rin Tin Tin (Rinty)—named for a little French puppet said to be good luck—back to Los Angeles after the war. The pup was extremely intelligent, and inspired by Strongheart, Duncan began to promote a career in show business for his dog. Rin Tin Tin's first starring role was in *Where the North Begins* (1923); soon the Rin Tin Tin movies became so popular that they were credited with saving the Warner Brothers studio from bankruptcy. (Ace the Wonder Dog was RKO studio's attempt to ride the amazing German shepherd movie star bandwagon.) From 1930–55, there were three different radio series starring Rin Tin Tin or one of his direct descendants. The original Rin Tin Tin died unexpectedly in August 1932, according to legend, in the arms of Jean Harlow, who was Lee Duncan's California neighbor. Lee Duncan, however, owned four of Rin Tin Tin's direct descendants, and they continued his performing legacy. During World War II, Duncan trained more than 5,000 German shepherds as military dogs at California's Camp Hahn. He willed the Rin Tin Tin line of dogs to Janietta Props, and her granddaughter, Daphne Hereford, continues to breed Rin Tin Tin descendants today—so you can still buy a direct descendant of Rin Tin Tin!

TOTO, AKA TERRY

Dorothy's dog in *The Wizard of Oz* was played by Terry, a Cairn terrier who had appeared in 13 previous movies, including *Fury* (1936), with Spencer Tracy, and *Bright Eyes* (1934), with Shirley Temple. Her trainer was Carl Spitz. Terry had a broken foot during the *Wizard of Oz* filming, when she was stepped on by one of the Wicked Witch of the West's guards. Nevertheless, Terry was said to be very fond of Margaret Hamilton, who played the Wicked Witch of the West. Prior to filming, Terry spent two weeks living at Judy Garland's home so that she could bond with the mercurial star. Terry was paid just $125 a week for her role in the movie, although, as she notes in *I, ToTo* her (ghost-written, by Willard Carroll) 2001 autobiography, she is in almost every scene, and is instrumental in two important plot devices: she escapes from the witch's castle where Dorothy is imprisoned—"Run, Toto, run!"—to fetch the Scarecrow, Cowardly Lion, and Tin Man to the rescue, and it is Toto who pulls aside the curtain to reveal that the great Wizard of Oz is nothing but a shrunken old man pulling the levers of a vast smokescreen machine.

TINSELTOWN STARS
CONTINUED

 ASTA

Asta, the legendary canine star of *The Thin Man* movies with William
Powell and Myrna Loy, was played by a wire-haired fox terrier originally named
Skippy. However, after his success in the first movie, his name was expediently
changed to Asta, and the pooch was said to answer to both. Asta/Skippy was
owned by Henry East and trained by East and Rudd Weatherwax (see page 65),
the trainer of Lassie (see page 64) and Old Yeller. From 1934–47, six *The Thin
Man* movies were made. Skippy/Asta was in the first two; afterward, Skippy's
descendants played the role. Skippy/Asta himself also starred in *The Awful
Truth* (1937), as the object of a custody dispute between Cary Grant and Irene
Dunne, and the classic *Bringing Up Baby* (1938), with Grant and Katharine
Hepburn. Skippy even got to play himself as a ghost dog in the movie *Topper
Takes a Trip* (1939). *The Thin Man* movies were based on an original novel by
Dashiell Hammett; in the novel, Asta is a miniature schnauzer, not a wire-haired
fox terrier. The breed switch has never been explained, but it led to a rash of
popularity for wire fox terriers in the late 1930s and early 1940s.

BENJI

The original Benji was a male terrier mix named Higgins, adopted by trainer Frank Inn from a shelter in Burbank, California. Higgins was 15 when he first played Benji; Higgins' first acting job was in the television series *Petticoat Junction*. Higgins was famous for his ability to project emotion and learn complicated routines, and he was particularly good at acting without requiring a lot of eye contact with his off-screen trainer. One critic commented, "This hound could play Hamlet!" Benji/Higgins was the second dog to be inducted into the Animal Actor's Hall of Fame; Lassie was the first. The aging Higgins retired soon after the first Benji movie and his role was taken over by his daughter, Benjean. Her ear tips were dyed black so that she would look more like Higgins.

The Benji franchise has produced seven movies, four television specials, and one television series; the movies have grossed over $600 million. Joe Camp wrote and produced all of the Benji movies independently. Their success has made him one of the most successful independent movie makers of all time.

Since the original Benji, four different dogs have played Benji. The most recent was adopted by Joe Camp from the Humane Society of South Mississippi. Camp noted that the story of the original Benji's adoption was estimated by the American Humane Society to be responsible for over 1 million adoptions; for the most recent Benji "star search" in shelters across the country, Camp made a concerted effort to generate favorable publicity for shelter dog adoption. The current Benji, who is blind in one eye as a result of cataract surgery, makes her home with Camp and his wife. Camp is also active in equine welfare and the next Benji movie, *Mustang Lost*, features Benji in partnership with a horse.

PETE THE PUP

The good natured dog of the *Our Gang* comedies was an American Staffordshire terrier, otherwise known as a pit bull. That famous enormous black ring around Pete's eye was makeup, and the ring had a tendency to migrate from one eye to the other over the years. The original Pete was played by Pal the Wonder Dog, who also starred as Tige in the *Buster Brown* 1920s series of live-action short movies based on the *Buster Brown* comic strips. After Pal died, trainer Harry Lucenay drafted Pal's son, Lucenay's Peter, to fill the role (nepotism seems to be an accepted practice in the world of canine movie and television stars!) Later, Lucenay himself was fired and producer Hal Roach used a variety of unrelated dogs to play Pete.

TINSELTOWN STARS
CONTINUED

 LASSIE

The original Lassie was Pal, a collie left with the Weatherwaxes (see box) for training. Pal's owner never paid the bill, but told the Weatherwaxes to keep Pal instead. Since Pal was a small and not particularly fancy-looking collie, he was originally hired just as a stunt dog for *Lassie Come Home*, the first Lassie movie. An impressive show collie was hired to be the "on-screen" star. However, Pal showed so much intelligence and guts in scenes that required him to do tricky stunts, such as swim across a raging river, that before long, the show collie was sent back to the dog show circuit and Pal had a full-time job. All subsequent Lassies have been direct descendants of Pal and all have been males, because male collies are larger and do not shed their coats seasonally as do females.

The original Lassie story was adapted from a 1943 *Saturday Evening Post* short story by Eric Knight. In the story, Lassie is supposed to be a tricolor (a black, sable, and white collie), but the movie honchos thought that a sable-and-white collie would be flashier and so Lassie remained, the icon of the collie dog for generations.

 EDDIE

Eddie Spaghetti, because he had worms, was supposed to be one of the many minor characters on the sitcom *Frasier*; he belonged to Frasier's father, Martin, but the only person Eddie was known to obey was Frasier's ex-wife Lilith. At the height of the show's popularity, Moose, the Jack Russell terrier who played Eddie, received more fan mail than any of the human actors. Eddie was famous for his fixed stare, which he used to spook Frasier. Moose passed away in 2006 and was replaced by Enzo, his son and stunt double.

 HAPPY

On *The Jack LaLanne Show,* Happy was LaLanne's white shepherd who appeared with him on his 1950s' exercise show. Happy's name reflected the relentless good cheer of the indefatigable LaLanne.

JACK

In the book *Little House on the Prairie*, Jack was Laura Ingalls Wilder's bulldog; however, in the television series based on the book, Jack was a shaggy, white dog.

THE WEATHERWAX DOG-TRAINING DYNASTY

Rudd and Frank Weatherwax were brothers who arrived in Los Angeles, California, in 1913 and got into acting in a small way and dog training for the movies in a big way. The Weatherwax brothers, or their sons, have trained dogs for over 35 movies, including Asta, the fox terrier in the early *The Thin Man* movies; Lassie, for all of the *Lassie* movies through the 1980s; Toto, the Cairn terrier in the *Wizard of Oz*; Old Yeller in *Old Yeller*, as well as dogs for *The Yearling* (1946), *The Call of the Wild* (1935), and *Sounder* (1972).

The Weatherwaxes' favorite dog of all time was said not to be Lassie, but Rommy, a Cairn terrier and descendant of Toto in *The Wizard of Oz*. Rommy first appeared in 1942's *Reap the Wild Wind* and several movies following it, including *Without Love* (1945), with Lucille Ball and Katharine Hepburn.

YUKON KING

The Yukon Territory in the gold rush days of the 1890s was a wild, lawless place, but Sergeant William Preston of the Royal Canadian Mounted Police and his highly noble lead sled dog, Yukon King, were strong. They were uncorrupted. Like Batman and Robin of the tundra, they fought evildoers, and at the conclusion of every episode, Sergeant Preston would address his faithful dog and intone, "Well, King, this case is closed." *Challenge of the Yukon* was a radio show that ran from 1938 to 1947. King had been a husky puppy somehow lost in the wilderness (perhaps abandoned by careless mushers?) but lo! A wolf named Three Toes came upon the pup in the boreal forest and raised him as her own. Three Toes herself became a victim of the pitiless wilderness when she was attacked by a lynx; Sergeant Preston entered stage left in time to save Yukon King, but not Three Toes. So King had all the primal wisdom learned from his wolf foster mother, but a deep bond of loyalty to his rescuer, Sergeant Preston.

In fact, the radio King was not a real dog—his noble barks, growls, and howls were supplied by sound effects men Dewey Cole and Ted Johnstone. King's breed in the radio show was loosely defined. He was variously described as either a husky or a malamute in Preston's signature cry to his dog team, "On King! On you huskies!" or "On you malamutes!"—it depended on the episode. In the 1950s, when the radio show made the leap to television, a decision had to be made and King was played by a malamute.

CANINE SPOKESDOGS

THE RCA DOG
Nipper, the RCA dog, appeared on the record company label as the dog who listened at the megaphone for "his master's voice."

TIGE, THE BUSTER BROWN SHOE DOG
As baby boomers forced during their early years to wear sensible shoes may remember, all Buster Brown shoes came with a colorful sticker of Buster and Tige attached to the shoe's inner sole.

> "I'm Buster Brown, I live in a shoe;
> That's my dog Tige, he lives there too!"
> *(ad jingle for Buster Brown shoes)*

TACO BELL CHIHUAHUA
Named Gidget, the dog was discovered on the boardwalk at Venice Beach, California. She was placed in the ad, which is famous for the phrase "¡Yo quiero Taco Bell!" Gidget spent her retirement in La Grange, Texas.

MCGRUFF
This trenchcoat-wearing "Crime Dog" who looked like a bloodhound appeared in ads with his nephew, Scruff McGruff. Their slogan was "Take a bite out of crime."

SPUDS MCKENZIE
From 1987–89 the Anheuser-Busch "Bud Light" spokesdog was Spuds. The canine was introduced during a Superbowl ad; known as the "ultimate party animal," Spuds was often accompanied by a bevy of attractive human females known as the Spudettes. Ironically, Spuds, a white American bulldog with a patch over one eye, was actually a female bulldog named Honeytree Evil Eye!

DUKE
This golden retriever appeared in the Bush's Beans commercials. The owner, Jake Bush of the Bush Bean company, brags that Duke has never "spilled the beans" about secret family baked beans recipes; meanwhile, Duke wears an apron that says, "Make Me an Offer."

CANINE ARTWORK

LANDSEER PORTRAITS

Sir Edwin Henry Landseer (1802–73) was a painter celebrated during the Victorian era for his paintings of dogs and horses. Landseer had a great deal of popular success and reproductions of his work were commonly displayed in middle-class Victorian homes. Landseer was also a protégé of Queen Victoria

and the rest of the royal family, who frequently commissioned him to paint portraits of the queen, her children, her dogs, and her parrots. The dogs and parrots were sometimes featured alone, but if the children are portrayed, they are always in the company of a dog, presumably to add some interest! Landseer also did many engravings of common dogs caught in ordinary moments of their lives, such as in stable yards, doghouses, and in public doorways, as well as more "noble" portraits of distinguished dogs, such as the deerhounds of Sir Walter Scott. Landseer's sentimental portraits of black-and-white Newfoundland dogs guarding children they have apparently just saved from drowning were so popular that, even today, black-and-white Newfoundlands are known as Landseers.

YOYO, LUMP, AND PICASSO

YoYo was the Norwich terrier of David Duncan, the famous photojournalist and preferred photographer of Pablo Picasso. In October 1993, the four-month-old YoYo was abducted by Gypsies in Marseille, France, and held for ransom. The police held out little hope for rescue; however, the Gypsies loved the earthy Picasso, and because Duncan was Picasso's friend, they agreed to negotiate. The ransom was paid and YoYo was returned.

Duncan took many photos of Picasso at home with his beloved dachshund Lump. Lump was originally Duncan's dog, but Picasso adored Lump and adopted him; he later placed Lump into a suite of 45 paintings that reinterpreted Velázquez' famous painting *Las Meniñas* (1656). In the original painting, a mastiff appears in the foreground, but in all of his reinterpretations, Picasso replaces the mastiff with the dachshund Lump.

THE PAINTERLY DACHSHUND

It is not particularly artistic in appearance, but nonetheless the dachshund appears to be the favorite dog breed of painters. The following painters all owned dachshunds:

Michelangelo
Leonardo da Vinci
Rembrandt
Peter Paul Rubens
Pablo Picasso

Andy Warhol
Diego Rivera and
Frida Kahlo
Georgia O'Keeffe
David Hockney

CANINE PAINTINGS FROM *BEST IN SHOW: THE DOG IN ART FROM THE RENAISSANCE TO THE PRESENT*

Here is a selection of paintings from this recent traveling art exhibit.

Dogs in An Interior (1649), Paulus Potter (in the Dutch Baroque style)
Dog With A Bowl (1751), Jean-Baptiste Oudry (King Louis XIV of
    France employed Oudry to paint the royal hounds)
Les Petites Favoris (The Little Favorites), Anne Vallayer-Coster
    (a favorite painter of Queen Marie Antoinette)
Portrait of the Spaniel of the Infanta Maria Josefa de Bourbon (1763),
    Giovanni Battista Tiepolo
Portrait of a King Charles Spaniel (1778), Jean-Baptiste Marie Huet
Portrait of an Extraordinary Musical Dog, Philip Reinagle
Portrait of a Terrier, The Property of Owen Williams, Esq., M.P.
    (Jocko with a Hedgehog; 1828), Sir Edwin Henry Landseer
Attachment (1829), Sir Edwin Henry Landseer
Pug and Terrier (1875), John Sargeant Noble
A Lady of Quality (portrait of a borzoi), William Frank Calderon
Ginger (1976), Andy Warhol (a 4-foot/1.2-m tall painting of a
    cocker spaniel)
Dog Painting 22 (1995), David Hockney (a painting of dachshunds)

CHAPTER 4

Dogs of Lore and Legend

Sometimes it seems like dogs haunt us! In the old days, dogs slipped

about the edges of human villages, guiding us on otherworldly

hunts and seeming to be able to sense what we ourselves could not.

Their behavior gave rise to tales of dogs as portents of both luck

and disaster and assigned the dog its role as a psychopomp,

or conductor of souls.

DOGS IN MYTHOLOGY

U nlike cats, dogs are not as prominent in ancient folklore and legends and don't seem to be held in the same high esteem that was expressed toward cats. In fact, at times they were seen as unlucky (see page 82). In ancient Egypt, thousands of mummified cats have been found; however, while the occasional mummified dog has been discovered, they are rare. Dogs are seldom referred to in Christianity, Judaism, and Islam, although they do play a more important role in Greek mythology and in Chinese traditions.

 ## DOG-HEADED GOD OF THE DEAD

Anubis was the jackal- or dog-headed Egyptian god of the dead. Appropriately for a canine, Anubis was said by the Egyptians to be both guide and guardian of the dead (known as a psychopomp, or conductor of souls). The Egyptians preserved their dead with herbs because Anubis would judge each person with his sensitive canine nose; if a person smelled pure, he or she would be allowed to enter the Kingdom of the Dead. Like primitive dogs, Anubis was said to haunt the edges, a go-between of life and death. In fact, the very idea of the dog-headed god may have come from observing wild scavenger dogs haunting the edges of burial grounds.

 ## THE TALE OF THE DOG STAR

In Greek mythology, Maera was the hound of Icarius, a protégé of the wine god Dionysus. The god had taught Icarius how to make wine. While traveling, Icarius was killed by some shepherds. Worried about her father, his daughter, Erigone, set off with Maera to find him. The dog led Erigone to her father's grave, and both were so overwhelmed with grief that Erigone hung herself and Maera leaped off a cliff. When Dionysus heard the news, the god memorialized all three in the sky as the constellations Virgo (Erigone), Boötes (Icarius), and the dog star, Sirius (Maera).

SCORCHING SIRIUS

Sirius, the brightest star in the night sky, is known as the "dog star" because it appears in the constellation Canis Major, or big dog. The Latin name for Sirius is *canicula*, or "little dog." The ancient Romans used the phrase *caniculares dies,* or "dog days," to refer to the days when Sirius rose at sunrise in the northern hemisphere. Because these days are also usually the hottest of the summer, and because the star is so bright, the ancients thought Sirius added its heat to the sun; so the word Sirius also means "scorching." The ancients were said to sacrifice a brown dog at this time to appease the rage of Sirius.

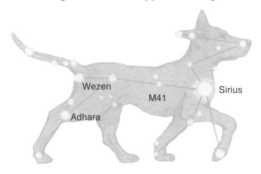

Wezen

M41

Sirius

Adhara

 ## FAITHFUL TO THE END

Argos was the faithful dog of Odysseus. The story of Argos in Homer's *Odyssey* can bring a tear to the eye of any dog lover—as it does to Odysseus himself. When Odysseus returned to Ithaca after 20 years of fighting in the Trojan War, only the frail Argos recognized Odysseus, even though he was in the disguise of a beggar. Bred by Odysseus as a noble hunting hound, during his absence, the once elegant Argos was forgotten and was reduced to a flea-bitten old dog lying on a dung heap. As soon as he saw Odysseus, Argos raised his head and wagged the tip of his tail. Odysseus recognized the dog and a tear dashed from his eye. However, Argos had already "passed into the darkness of death"; the one he has waited for during the last 20 years had finally returned. Odysseus had to hide his grief, because he was trying to disguise his identity. The moment when he turned aside in order not to be observed wiping away a tear is both low key, yet also one of the most pathetic vignettes in the *Odyssey*.

MORE ANCIENT CANINES

GUARD DOG

Cerberus was the three-headed (but some tales say 50-headed) hound of Hades from Greek myths. Cerberus guarded the gates of hell, allowing the dead to enter, but none to exit. Cerberus reputedly had a serpent for a tail and a mane of snakes.

BARKING MAD

Many legends claim that Hecuba, the Queen of Troy, turned into a dog. Each legend, however, tells a different tale of how this came to pass. One story has it that she was driven so mad by grief after the Trojan War and the deaths of her children Polydorus and Polyxena, that she began to bark like a dog.

A variation of the story says that Hecuba was given to Odysseus as a slave, but she snarled at him, whereupon the gods turned her into a dog with fiery eyes and she leaped from Odysseus' ship into the Aegean and disappeared. Still another variation says that after she avenged the death of her young son Polydorus (by having the sons of the king who had betrayed Polydorus killed), Agamemnon prophesized that Hecuba would be turned into a bitch and her tomb would be known as Cynos Sema, or dog's tomb.

WATCH DOG PAR EXCELLENCE

Kitmer was the dog of the Seven Sleepers, seven young men who were being persecuted for their Christianity during the reign of Emperor Decius, about 250 A.D. The young men fled to a cave, and on the way there they met a great dog that they tried to drive off. However, the dog spoke, saying "I love those who are dear to God, go to sleep, therefore, and I will guard you." The dog lay in the mouth of the cave and guarded the seven sleepers for 300 years without eating, moving, or sleeping. A version of the tale of the Seven Sleepers also appears in the Koran, and Kitmer is said in the Koran to be one of only three animals admitted by Mohammed to Paradise. (The others are the camel that the prophet Mohammed rode on during the flight from Mecca, and Balaam's Ass.)

DOG PROVERBS FROM AROUND THE WORLD

AFRICAN
A dog knows the places he is thrown food.

Do not call to a dog with a whip in your hand.

The lion does not turn around when a small dog barks.

BURMA
If a sane dog fights a mad dog, it's the sane dog's ear that is bitten off.

CHINA
Better to be a dog in times of peace than a human being in times of trouble.

One dog barks at something, the rest bark at him.

Out of a dog's mouth will never come ivory tusks.

The black dog gets the food, the white dog gets the blame.

DENMARK
An honest man is not the worse because a dog barks at him.

The dog's kennel is not the place to keep a sausage.

EGYPT
The barking of a dog does not disturb the man on a camel.

FINLAND
It is home to a dog after he has been there three nights.

GERMANY
The fatter the flea, the leaner the dog.

To live long, eat like a cat, drink like a dog.

JAPAN
If a man is great, even his dog will wear a proud look.

One dog yelping at nothing will set 10,000 straining at their collars.

POLAND
The greatest love is a mother's, then a dog's, then a sweetheart's.

PORTUGAL
The dog wags his tail, not for you, but for your bread.

RUSSIA
If you are a host to your guest, be a host to his dog, too.

SAUDI ARABIA
If you stop every time a dog barks, your road will never end.

TURKEY
A dog that intends to bite does not bare its teeth.

UNITED STATES
A good dog deserves a good bone.

CHINESE DOGS

The Chinese were among the first people to domesticate the dog, and China is where dogs were first bred as guard and hunting dogs, probably from the fifth or fourth millennium B.C. There were two species of Han hunting dogs: the slim greyhound used for hunting deer and the stockier mastiff, introduced to China by the ancient Turks. The Chinese mastiff was a powerful dog with a tail curled on its back that is similar to today's Pekingese and chow chow.

 THE DOG STAR

In Chinese mythology, Sirius is referred to as *tian gou xing,* the "heavenly dog star," who is said to have devoured the moon at the time of an eclipse.

 IN THE ELEVENTH HOUR

The dog is the eleventh sign of the Chinese zodiac. Legend has it that the animals had to swim across a river, and the winners would form the zodiac. The dog, one of the best swimmers, should had made it to the finishing line early on, but he found the fresh water in the river too much of a temptation and had a long bath. He managed to finish the race, but only in the penultimate position.

 CHINESE CREATION

In China, there are many creation stories about Pan Gu. This is one version of the legend among the Miao of southern China, who believe Pan Gu has a man's body and dog's head. In Heaven, King Gao Xin was the god in charge of the earth and he owned a beautiful spotted dog. He reared him on a plate (*pan* in Chinese) inside a gourd (*hu*), so the dog was called Pan Gu. There was a great feud between King Gao Xin and another god, King Fang. King Gao Xin had declared that if someone brought him the head of King Fang, that person would be rewarded Gao's daughter in marriage. Yet, not a single man was brave enough to try because all were afraid of King Fang's soldiers. However, Pan Gu heard the declaration and he slipped out of the palace and ran to King Fang, where he approached him, wagging his tail. Fang thought King Gao Xin was near his end because his dog had left him, so he held a banquet. Fang drank too much, and when he went to bed, Pan Gu bit off his head and brought it back to his master. Pan Gu was rewarded with fresh meat, but he refused to eat for three days. When the king asked why his dog wouldn't eat, Pan Gu began to speak, "Just cover me with your golden bell and in seven days and seven nights I'll become a man." The King did as he said, but on the sixth day, the princess peeped under the bell. Although Pan Gu's body had turned into a man's body, he still had a dog's head—and because the bell was lifted, that is how he remained. When he married the princess, the couple moved to the earth, and their offspring are the ancestors of mankind.

 ## THE DRAGON DOG

Another legend tells of Pan Hu, a striped dragon dog, who destroys a rival ruler for the emperor after his ministers refused to do so. Pan Hu had been promised a lady of the court in marriage if his mission was a success, and so the couple was married. They were given provisions but had to "stay in the wilderness always." They had twelve children, and each of these was made the head of a lineage. These are the descendents of the Yao people, an ethnic group who by decree were free from taxation and other duties to the emperor.

 ## THE LION DOG

The dog of Fo, or lion dog, is a mythical Chinese hybrid lion/guard dog often depicted as a guardian at the entrance of Buddhist temples and shrines. During the Han Dynasty (207 B.C.–A.D. 220), gifts of lions were sent from Persia and India to China, where they were kept in imperial zoos. In Buddhism, lions symbolize power and strength, and the symbolism was soon adopted by the Chinese, whose word for "Buddha" is *Fo*. The lion was an uncommon sight in China, so their artists depicted it more like the dog that was known to them. Hence, the dogs of Fo became temple guardians somewhat like the Buddhist guardian lion. They have been adopted to also guard homes, businesses, and even government buildings, repelling evil spirits and demons.

MEDIEVAL DOGS

 ## THE CHRIST CARRIER

Saint Christopher, known for carrying Jesus across a swift river, is the patron saint of travelers. He is often portrayed in Byzantine icons with a dog's head. He is said to have been a member of the North African tribe, the Marmaritae (from present-day Libya). Baptized by Peter of Antioch, Saint Christopher was martyred for his faith, but because he was said in early Greek and Roman accounts to have come from a land of "cannibals and dog-headed peoples," the iconographic portrayals of him with a dog's head persist. This myth of the Marmaritae is thought to have originated because baboons were mistaken for dog-headed people.

 ## SAINT HUBERT AND THE HOUNDS

The eldest son of the Duke of Aquitaine, Saint Hubert of Liege had a conversion experience while hunting stags. He had a vision of a stag with a crucifix between its antlers, so he gave up his heedless hunting ways and studied for the priesthood. During an outbreak of rabies in France and Belgium, Saint Hubert set up a refuge for all the dogs he could find, marking each with the sign of the cross on its forehead, which was believed to confer immunity to rabies. Following his death in 727, the monks in Ardennes renamed the Flemish hound, which Saint Hubert had brought from the South of Gaul, the Saint Hubert hound. Today, Saint Hubert is the patron saint of hydrophobia (yes, it's true, rabies has a patron saint) and is often depicted in iconography as a young courtier with two hounds. Saint Hubert has given his name to several modern kennel clubs, such as Belgium's Société Royale Saint Hubert.

 ## THE PATRON SAINT OF DOGS

Saint Roch, born in 1295 in Montpellier, France, is the patron saint of dogs. Born to wealth, Saint Roch gave up his noble title so that he could go on a pilgrimage to Rome and care for plague victims. When he contracted the plague himself, he retreated to a forest to suffer alone, but a dog from a nearby manor house befriended Saint Roch, brought him food, and licked his wounds. When Roch recovered, he took the dog and went back to his home, but everyone had died. He himself was so disfigured that he was thought to be an impostor and was imprisoned. Saint Roch and his dog spent the rest of their lives caring for other prisoners. Saint Roch died in 1327.

A FAITHFUL FRIEND

Although Guinefort was a greyhound, a knight left his infant son in his dog's care while he went hunting. The knight returned to find an overturned cradle and the greyhound with a bloody jaw. Leaping to conclusions, despite his former trust of the dog, the knight slew Guinefort; however, as he drew his sword and accomplished the precipitous and dastardly deed, the knight heard a baby cry. Turning over the cradle, he discovered his son and a dead snake! Guinefort had saved the infant from the snake, overturning the cradle in the melee. The knight, filled with grief and guilt, dropped poor Guinefort down a well, covered the well, and planted trees, making a holy well and shrine to his dog.

Guinefort was seen as a saint by locals, who appealed to him for the protection of babies. The Catholic Church tried to prohibit the worship of Guinefort—after all, he was a dog—but the cult persisted. The Church claimed that far from praying for the protection of babies, babies were sacrificed at the holy well.

There is also a Welsh version of this legend. In that story Guinefort is called Gelert, and he is an Irish wolfhound or Scottish deerhound. The knight's name is Llewellyn, and the creature who menaces the baby is a wolf not a snake.

MORE MEDIEVAL DOGS

DEVOTED DOG
Hodain was the hound of Sir Tristan in the tragic Medieval romance Tristan and Isolde. Hodain lapped at the cup, which contained the fateful love potion that the two lovers drank, and ever after Hodain was obsequiously faithful.

A DOG'S LIFE IN CAMELOT
King Arthur's dog, Cavall (oddly, the word means "horse"), was a hunting hound "of deepest mouth," referring to his distinctive bay, which Guinevere listened for whenever Arthur was out hunting. Legend says that Cavall left his footprint in a stone, and, to preserve it, Arthur built a stone cairn around the footprint-imprinted stone. Although men tried to carry the footprint stone away with them, the next day it always reappeared on the cairn.

SAME DOG, THREE STORIES
Luath is the ancient Irish hero Cuchullin's dog in Ossian's epic *Fingal*. In Irish, *luath* means "swift" or "fleet." Luath was the name of one of the Scottish poet Robert Burns' favorite dogs; afer Luath was killed while out wandering, Burns memorialized him a poem, *The Twa Dogs*. Luath is also the name of the Labrador retriever in Sheila Burnford's canine epic, *The Incredible Journey*.

FIONN'S HOUNDS
Bran and Sceolang (gray dog) were the two hunting dogs of the great Irish warrior and hunter Fionn mac Cumhaill. The dogs are celebrated in many stories for their wisdom. In the Irish version, Bran and Sceolang are the children of Fionn's sister Uirne, who had been turned into a dog by her husband's jilted lover, Illann. Uirne was restored to her human form, but her children remained canines.

Bran is preferred by Fionn and is a swift runner able to overtake geese in flight. Bran and Sceolang bring a young doe to Fionn's fortress; the doe is released from enchantment to become Fionn's beloved Sadb, the mother of his son Oisin. Later, she is lured from the fortress and becomes a deer again; then Fionn will allow only Bran and Sceolang to hunt because they know Sadb and will do her no harm. Bran and Sceolang find the infant Oisin in the forest.

Fionn is finally forced to kill Bran when she is hunting a fawn, evidently the transformed Sadb who she has not recognized. Fionn calls first to the fawn and then to Bran to run through his legs; when Bran passes, Fionn crushes her between his knees. Irish tradition has Bran buried at Cranawaddy (literally *carn an mhadra*, or "cairn of the dog"), a cairn near Ometh, County Louth. Lough Brin in County Kerry is thought to be named after Bran. Two bronze statues of Irish wolfhounds, said to be of Bran and Sceolang, stand in the medieval village of Kildare in Ireland.

The origin of Fionn's hounds is told differently in Ireland and Scotland. In the Scottish Gaelic version, the two dogs are unrelated to Fionn and are monstrous wild dogs that are won in a contest with a baby-eating predator.

DOG BITE CURE

The sure and sovereign remedy for them that are bitten by a mad dog was revealed by way of Oracle—to wit, the root of a wild rose, called the sweet Brier or Eglantine.

And there are some again, who burn the hairs of the same mad dog's tail, and convey their ashes handsomely in some tent of lint into the wound.

PLINY THE ELDER, A.D. 23–79, ROMAN SCHOLAR

DOGGY SUPERSTITIONS

Dogs, it was believed, could sense supernatural forces and see ghosts and other spirits that humans couldn't see. A dog's howling and whimpering was often thought to be a warning of a change of fortune.

LUCKY DOG

If a stray dog follows you home in China, it is thought to be a sign of impending wealth.

In England, meeting a spotted or black-and-white dog on the way to a business appointment is believed to be lucky.

A newborn baby licked by a dog will always be a fast healer.

A dog eating grass is said to be a sign of rain to come.

In Scotland, a strange dog turning up at your door means a new friendship.

Three white dogs together are a sign of good luck.

BAD DOG

In many parts of the world, a black dog is considered an evil omen, especially if it crosses your path.

A dog howling outside the door at night is unlucky—and if a sick person is inside, it is thought he or she will die, especially if a dog is driven away but then returns.

Some card players believe that playing with a dog in the room leads to arguments.

Dogs are unlucky according to fishermen, and many won't even mention "dog" while at sea—let alone allow one onboard.

DOGGY IDIOMS

SAYING	MEANING
As sick as a dog	To be very sick
Like a dog with two tails	To be really happy
Call off the dogs	Stop criticizing
The dog days	The hottest days in summer
Dog eat dog	When someone will do anything to get ahead
A dog in the manger	Holding onto something you don't want to keep it from others
Dog tired	Very tired
Every dog has its day	Everyone is successful at some time in their lives
Fight like cat and dog	To argue violently all the time
Go to the dogs	To become less successful
Not have a dog's chance	You don't have any chance
Hot dog	An exclamation of joy; or to show off
It's a dog's life	Something that is difficult
Let sleeping dogs lie	Don't talk about past problems
Put on the dog	To try to impress beyond your financial means
Raining cats and dogs	Heavy rain
A shaggy dog story	A long story with a silly ending
The tail wagging the dog	To give something more influence than something that is important
There's life in the old dog yet	Although old, still lively
Three dog night	A really cold night (Inuits would sleep with three dogs to keep warm)
Throw someone to the dogs	To protect yourself by allowing someone else to be attacked
The top dog	The most important person
Work like a dog	Be a hard worker
You can't teach an old dog new tricks	It's difficult to change someone already set in their ways.

HELLHOUNDS

Hounds from hell have a long history. When you accuse your black Labrador, who has just shredded your new Manolos, of being a hound from hell, you should know that you are associating him with a fearsome and ancient tradition.

DIP: In Catalan myth, Dip is the devil's black hairy dog. He is lame in one leg, and sucks people's blood.

MOODY DHU: On the Isle of Man, a black spaniel that appeared at the lighting of the torches in Peel Castle, and disappeared at daybreak. During excavations of the castle in 1871, the bones of a thirteenth-century bishop were reportedly found with those of a dog at his feet.

BLACK SHUCK: A huge black dog with flaming eyes "like saucers" said to appear at night on the dark roads and byways of East Anglia, England. The name Shuck probably derives from the Old English word *scucca,* meaning "demon," and it is said that those who see the beast are destined to meet a sudden death. In 1577, Black Shuck attacked two Suffolk churches on a single day, leaving several parishoners dead and scorch marks on the north door of Blytheburgh Church. The burned wood can still be seen today. It is also known as Old Shuck, Gurt Dog, Devil's Dandy, Guytrash, and Skriker.

BARGHEST: A demonic black dog of Yorkshire, England, said to haunt the snickleways (small winding paths and side streets, crossroads, and country lanes) of the city of York and its surrounding countryside. The Barghest is featured in the game Dungeons and Dragons. The origin of the name is obscure, although in Germany, the "Bier-gheist" is said to be the spirit of the funeral bier.

GWYLLGI: The "Dog of Darkness" in Wales is an apparition of a mastiff with foul breath and fiery eyes.

CU SITH: Literally, "fairy dog," a legendary shaggy dog of the Scottish highlands. The size of a cow, the creature had a shaggy green coat and a long braided tail. Although usually a silent hunter, the Cu Sith (pronounced "coo shee") sometimes gave three terrible barks. This was a sign to farmers to lock up their wives, because the Cu Sith stole fertile women and abducted them to fairy mounds to supply milk for the Sidhe, or fairy children.

:paw: GARMR: In Norse mythology, Garmr (similar to Cerberus) guards the entrance to "Helheim," the Norse realm of the dead. Garmr has four eyes and a chest drenched with blood, and lives in Gnipa Cave. Anyone who had given bread to the poor could appease him with Hel cake.

MORE RECENT HELLHOUNDS

The Hound of the Baskervilles, written by Sir Arther Conan Doyle, was a Sherlock Holmes story first serialized in *The Strand* magazine in 1901–2. It tells the story of hellraising landowner Sir Hugo Baskerville, who was supposedly killed by "a great, black beast, shaped like a hound" that now haunts his descendants. Conan Doyle probably based the hound on the Black Shuck legend; he is known to have vacationed in East Anglia, where he may have heard the story.

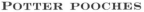

POTTER POOCHES

:paw: THE GRIM: In *Harry Potter and the Prisoner of Azkaban,* Harry's movements are followed by a scary black dog that he doesn't recognize. Eventually, his Divination teacher, Professor Trelawney, enlightens him that the creature is the Grim—a giant spectral dog that haunts churchyards and is a terrible omen of death.

:paw: FLUFFY: The first guardian of the Sorcerer's Stone, Fluffy has three heads and can only be handled safely by Hagrid.

:paw: FENRIR GREYBACK: A Death Eater werewolf who bites Remus Lupin and Bill Weasley.

SOUTHERN DOG

The "blue dog" paintings of well-known Louisiana artist George Rodrigue are based on the Cajun legend of a ghost dog known as the loup-garou. Rodrigue's first paintings of this legend featured gray-blue dogs with glowing red eyes, set against a background of Louisiana cemeteries. As his paintings have evolved, the dogs now have yellow eyes. The emphasis on glowing fiery eyes and cemeteries suggests that the loup-garou is another version of the devil dog or hellhound legend.

CHAPTER 5

Will Work for Biscuits

In their long association with humans, dogs seem to have absorbed a little of our work hard/play hard ethic. Dogs able to put their innate talents to the test, such as hunting or herding dogs, are joyful workers and inspiring to watch; however, dogs have also shouldered darker and heavier burdens for their human friends—at war and in rescue.

COMPETITIVE DOGS

Few dog breed descriptions read "This dog was bred to sleep on the couch, dig up the yard, raid the trash, and drag his cranky human partner on a tour of neighborhood sidewalks several times a day." No, most breeds "profiles" proudly claim that once upon a time the breed had a purpose in life, and that the modern pedigreed pooch is more than just a pretty face. Many purebred dog clubs now promote activities to let dogs rediscover their roots.

CANINE "FREESTYLE" COMPETITIONS

A mélange adapted from traditional AKC Obedience Trials and equine dressage musical "kurs," or freestyle dressage performances, canine freestyles are choreographed dog/human obedience displays set to music. Freestyles are intended to demonstrate not only that the dog is trained, but the "joyful relationship" of the dog/human handler–trainer obedience team. Freestyles are judged on the degree of "interactive attention," or sustained visual contact and engagement between the handler and the dog.

THE SPORTING DOG

Flyball is a dog sport at which hyper dogs excel. If you have a dog who considers a brisk walk around the block as merely a meager warmup, consider joining a flyball team. Invented in California in the 1970s, flyball is a relay race with four dog teams. The dogs race down a 51-foot (15.5-m) course, where they jump four hurdles and pounce on a spring-loaded box that ejects a tennis ball. The dog catches the ball and races back down the course over the hurdles, then it's the next dog's turn. A good team can complete a flyball round in 25 seconds, and the world record is 15.43 seconds. It takes several months for dogs to learn flyball and to perfect their techniques.

WHAT A TEAM

Team Ghost Riders is a pack of border collies, based in Gainesville, Florida, who are ridden by capuchin monkeys wearing cowboy outfits. Together, the monkeys and the dogs put on sheepherding exhibitions throughout the United States.

IN SEARCH OF A JOB

COMPETITION	BREED	THE CHALLENGE
Earth dog trials	Dachshunds, small terriers	Dog enters the tunnel (den) in the ground, negotiates a tunnel, and "works" (barks, growls at, and otherwise threatens and pesters) a rat in a cage; tests gameness and prey drive.
Field trials/ hunting dog tests	Pointers, setters, retrievers, spaniels	Various trials to test the dog's nose, bird finding ability, hunting drive, retrieving instinct (for retrievers), pointing instinct (setters and pointers), quartering pattern (spaniels), and manners on game (for trained dogs in the more formal and competitive field trials).
Mushing	Huskies, malamutes; any breed or crossbred dog (in nonAKC events)	Teams of dogs pull a sled with a handler (person) on the runners; the team that completes the marked course in the fastest time wins.
Lure coursing	Greyhounds, sighthounds	The dogs chase quarry—jackrabbits or small game, or in lure coursing, a mechanical lure—across a course, some with jumps; tests agility, drive, and intensity.
Sheepdog trials	Herding dogs	Tests a herding dog's ability to gather sheep from a pasture, as well as move, sort, and pen the sheep.

DISK DOG

Also known as Frisbee dog, disk dog pits dog against dog in a display of Frisbee-manipulation skills. The game began on August 5, 1974, when college student Alex Stein and his extraordinary dog, Ashley Whippet, leaped onto a baseball field during a game between the L.A. Dodgers and the Cincinnati Reds. The game was being broadcast nationally from Dodger Stadium. Bewildered spectators watched in amazement as the pair put on an astonishing eight-minute display of Frisbee-catching tricks, featuring 9-foot (2.7-m) leaps into the air. This gave birth to a popular sport, which now includes a competition held every year.

The rules of disk dog are simple. In short-distance competitions, teams (which consist of one dog and its owner) are judged on how many catches they can field in a set amount of time over varying distances. In long-distance competitions, the prize is awarded for the longest catch.

In the popular freestyle events, dogs perform choreographed displays of Frisbee-catching tricks, often using several disks. The teams are judged in a similar fashion to disciplines such as figure skating or skateboarding—according to the difficulty and aesthetic appeal of their skills. One of the most common features of freestyle competitions are very fast repetitive catches or flips of the disk.

THE POWER OF FAITH

The cute Labrador-chow crossbreed Faith was born with a deformity that meant both of her front legs had to be amputated. However, that didn't stop her claiming a place in the hearts of the Stringfellow family of Oklahoma City, who set about the task of teaching Faith to walk—on two legs! After putting Faith on a skateboard to get her used to the sensation of motion, the family gradually taught her to stand upright, hop, and eventually walk, using just her hind legs. Faith, who stood at nearly 3 feet (91 cm) tall, appeared on numerous television shows, and led a full and happy life until her sad death in 2014.

DISK DOG WORLD CHAMPIONS

YEAR	OWNER	DOG'S NAME
1977	Alex Stein	Ashley Whippet
1978	Jim Strickler	Dink
1979	Jim Strickler	Dink
1980	Frank Allen	Kona
1981	Bob Cox	Belmond
1982	Bill Murphy	Bouncin' Boo
1983	Bill Murphy	Bouncin' Boo
1984	Peter Bloeme	Whirlin' Wizard
1985	Bill Murphy	Bouncin' Boo
1986	Chris Barbo	Kato
1987	Jeff Gabel	Casey
1988	Jeff Gabel	Casey
1989	Jeff Perry	Gilbert
1990	Lou McCammon	Scooter
1991	Ron Ellis	Maggy
1992	Lou McCammon	Scooter
1993	Gary Suzuki	Soarin' Sam
1994	Gary Suzuki	Soarin' Sam
1995	Gary Suzuki	Soarin' Sam
1996	Pon Saradeth	Owen Boy
1997	Melissa Heeter	Ariel Asah
1998	Bob Evans	Luke
1999	Ken Cooper	Gabby
2000	Bob Evans	Nick
2001	David Bootes	Chico
2002	Chuck Middleton	Donnie
2003	Bob Evans	Nick
2004	Bob Evans	Nick
2005	Steve Malmlov	Foster
2006	Yoshihiro Ishida	Rusty

SHEEPDOGS

The first official sheepdog trials were held in 1873. They took place in Bala, Merionethshire, Wales.

Traditional commands used in sheepdog trials:
Away to me, or away: Go counterclockwise around the stock
Come by: Go clockwise around the stock
Lie down: Stop and lie down
There: Stop and wait for the next command
That'll do: Stop working, return to handler
Come, come here, here: Move to handler
Walk up: Move toward the stock
Get back, get out: Move away from the stock
Easy, steady: Go slower
Balance: Position yourself to keep the stock moving toward the handler.

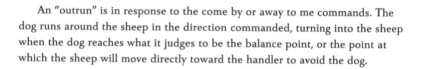

An "outrun" is in response to the come by or away to me commands. The dog runs around the sheep in the direction commanded, turning into the sheep when the dog reaches what it judges to be the balance point, or the point at which the sheep will move directly toward the handler to avoid the dog.

THE HYPNOTIC EYE

This is the term for the "strong eye," or bold, intent stare, that some strains of sheepdog, in particular border collies, use to "magically" control a herd of sheep. The strong eye can sometimes become the "sticky eye"; this refers to when sheepdogs become so fixed on staring that they neglect to move when they should and lose control of the sheep. In this case, the strong herding eye almost morphs into a point like that of a pointing dog. "Loose-eyed" sheepdogs do not employ the intense stare in the same way; they tend to crouch less and instead use their bodies to herd, blocking, bumping, and pushing, and focusing on the herd as a whole instead of a single fixed point in the herd as do strong-eyed sheepdogs. Traditional Scotch collies, the progenitor of the modern rough-coated collie, were more likely to be "loose eyed." Many feel that the "hypnotic eye" was developed as a preferred "style" for sheepdog trials.

TRUFFLE DOG

Truffle hunting is a skill that a dog can learn without much trouble, and it is a valuable one, because truffles sell for approximately $350 to $1000 per pound. Pigs, which have excellent noses and a decided taste for truffles, excel at rooting out the valuable fungi, but they are apt to eat the prize and are difficult to transport to the truffle hunting ground. Therefore, dogs are preferred. In France, the elite poodle, fittingly enough, is the traditional breed for hunting out this gourmet favorite, although any eager dog has the potential to do the job. In 1991, the Italian Kennel Club recognized a breed that resembles a crossbred poodle, called the lagotto Romagnolo, specifically for truffle hunting.

Truffles have a pungent odor that has been likened to an old gym sock. They are found in the fall, in damp forests, growing underground in symbiosis with the roots of certain species of trees (pines, beeches, birches, hickories, oaks, and hazelnuts). Dogs are trained by teaching them to sniff out buried pieces of smelly Gorgonzola cheese (or occasionally a bit of real truffle protected in a leather bag), then rewarded with a piece of bread when they locate and scratch at the ground above the prize. Once the dog finds the truffle and begins to dig, he is hurriedly shoved out of the way and his human partner finishes the job, before the dog scratches the valuable fungus with its claws. Experienced truffle dogs are so valuable that they are vulnerable to kidnapping in some parts of France and Italy.

STAGE FRIGHT

In 1992, Diana, a truffle dog of fabled skill, was scheduled to do a command performance onstage at Carnegie Hall in Manhattan before a tense crowd of interested gourmets and restaurateurs. Truffles were hidden under ficus trees onstage; however, like many a diva before her, Diana suffered from nerves. She hid under the voluminous evening skirts of her owner and refused to hunt.

A FEW RECORD BREAKERS

 ## PEAK-CONQUERING POOCH

A golden retriever named Rubia made headlines in 2004 when she climbed to the summit of Aconcagua, the highest mountain in the western hemisphere. Wearing goggles, boots, and a specially designed snowsuit, Rubia scaled the 22,834-foot (6,960-m) peak, which lies in Argentina, with two Spanish climbers. The intrepid two-year-old had been trained for the attempt since she was just seven months old. Incredibly, Rubia may not have been the first dog to successfully climb the mountain. Unconfirmed reports claim that a stray dog accompanied a group of Austrian and German climbers to the summit a decade earlier.

 ## LAST-ACTION CANINE

Surely one of the most fearless and death-defying dogs of recent years, a Jack Russell terrier called Part-Ex gained fame in 2000 when he made it into the *Guinness Book of Records*—as the dog who had participated in the most extreme sports. Part-Ex's favorite activities were said to include kayaking, surfing, and "coastlining"—a hobby that involved walking the clifftop paths near his home in Wales and leaping into the sea if the path reached a dead end!

OTHER RECORD BREAKERS

In 1998, Duke, a border collie–Australian shepherd mix, made it into the *Guinness Book* for his ability to climb 13 tires piled on top of each other, reaching 9 feet 4 inches (28.5 m) high, all just to reach a toy hidden at the top!

In September 2004, Striker, a border collie, set a record in Quebec by unwinding a (nonelectric) car window in just 11.34 seconds.

Cinderella, a greyhound, jumped 66 inches (167.6 cm) at the Purina Dog Chow Incredible Dog Challenge in October 2003.

In 1963, Charlie, a husky, set a record by moving a 3,142-pound (1,425-kg) sled.

Chota Peg, an American cocker spaniel, logged 13 years (1952–69) and 2 million nautical miles at sea.

DOGS IN SPACE

Some dogs never get to do anything special—they aren't even permitted to sleep on the couch, or eat ice cream. However, between 1957 and 1966, several dogs in the Soviet Union were selected for the space program, giving them the dubious privilege of being the first living creatures to go into space.

Albina and *Tsyganka* didn't quite make it into space, but they deserve a mention. The two dogs were blasted up 53 miles (85 km) to the edge of Earth's atmosphere to test spacesuits in unpressurized cabins. The pair landed on Earth safely, in their ejection seats.

Laika ("Barker" in Russian), a stray female mongrel from Moscow, went into space on November 3, 1957, on *Sputnik 2,* making her the very first living creature to go into orbit. In the United States she was also known as Muttnik, the nickname given to her by the press. Sadly, Laika died in space from stress and overheating, although the Russians claimed it was due to poisoned food or lack of oxygen.

Belka ("Squirrel") and *Strelka* ("Little Arrow") went into space on *Sputnik 5* on August 19, 1960.

They were the first dogs to survive an orbital flight. Their mission also included 40 mice, 2 rats, a gray rabbit, flies, and some plants and fungi. All returned to Earth after a day in orbit. Strelka even went on to have a litter of six puppies, one of which was presented to President John F. Kennedy and adored by the president's daughter Caroline.

Chernushka ("Blackie") went into space on *Sputnik 9* on March 9, 1961. Other animal passengers included a few mice and a guinea pig. They all returned safely, as did the dummy cosmonaut—which was a wooden mannequin.

Zvezdochka ("Little Star"), named by Yuri Gagarin, went on a one-orbit mission on *Sputnik 10* on March 25, 1961. It was the final test flight before Gagarin became the first man in space.

GUIDE DOGS FOR THE BLIND

Dogs have informally assisted the blind for generations, but the first formal guide dog training program in the United States was not established until 1929. Dorothy Harrison Eustis, a wealthy Philadelphian who lived in Switzerland, had become interested in some short-lived German programs to train dogs for the blind and she began to train her own German shepherds for the purpose, following the German model. In 1927, she wrote an article about the training process for the *Saturday Evening Post*. The article came to the attention of Morris Frank, a young blind man from Tennessee. He traveled to Switzerland to work with Mrs. Eustis and when he returned to the United States in January 1929, he set up The Seeing Eye with funds from Mrs. Eustis. Frank's guide dog was a female German shepherd, Buddy. By the end of 1929, 17 people received guide dogs from The Seeing Eye school. In 1931, the school relocated to Morristown, NJ, where it remains today.

TWO SUPER GUIDE DOGS

Two golden Labradors, both guide dogs for the blind, shepherded their humans through hellish conditions to safety when the World Trade Center was attacked on September 11, 2001. Roselle and Dorado guided Michael Hingson and Omar Rivera, respectively, down more than 70 flights of stairs, through smoke and terrible heat, to safety. What more can be said about the incredible faithfulness of dogs? Rivera actually released his dog, thinking that he himself was doomed, but perhaps the dog could escape. "I ruffled his head and told him to go," Rivera said later. However, Dorado stayed with his owner. "Dorado kept nudging me down, step by step." Roselle and Dorado both received the Dickin Medal (see pages 104–5) for their heroism.

THE SAINT BERNARD

This gentle giant of a dog, which is the Swiss national dog, has earned a reputation as a rescue dog. Napoleon is just one of the travelers who has reported on lives being saved by the "barry dog," as it was known when the French emperor was in the Alps. Barry (1800–14) was a seventeenth-century Saint Bernard said to have rescued a monk who fell down a crevasse as a party of monks labored though the St. Bernard Pass, located at 8,100 feet (2,469 m) above sea level in the Alps between Italy and Switzerland. Legend says that Barry saved over 40 lives.

The hospice of St. Bernard honors his memory by always keeping a dog named Barry. Dogs were first kept at the hospice between 1660–70. The first written reference to the dogs was in 1703 by a Prior Balu, who wrote that the hospice cook had developed an exercise wheel for the dogs; when a dog was exercised on the wheel, a cooking spit was rotated.

Barry is memorialized by a monument near the entrance of the Cimitière des Chiens (a pet cemetery) outside Paris, but his body is preserved in the Natural History Museum of Switzerland. The preserved Barry is a large dog, but much smaller than the modern Saint Bernard. The original Barry weighed about 99 pounds (45 kg); today's Saint Bernards weigh closer to 143–187 pounds (65–85 kg), showing the tendency of show breeders to increase the size of breeds that they promote. When the original Barry was mounted in 1814, he was posed in a meek attitude to symbolize his dedication to service. However, when he was refurbished in 1923, he was posed in a proud, upstanding manner and his skull was altered to make the dog seem more imposing.

HUSKY HEROES

During the famous 1925 serum relay, known as The Great Race of Mercy, relay teams of approximately 150 sled dogs delivered diphtheria antitoxin to Nome, Alaska, to combat a serious diptheria epidemic. The dog sled relay teams completed the run in a record breaking 5½ days, traveling 674 miles (1,085 km) in extreme arctic temperatures, braving blizzards and hurricane force winds. Many of the dogs died. The serum run was headline news of the day and made a gripping story on radio, the high-tech media of the time. Today, the Iditarod sled dog race commemorates that grueling serum run. Togo and Balto were two dogs that survived the run and they became well known.

Balto, a jet black husky with white markings, was already 12 years old when he served as a lead dog in the serum run. The real Balto appeared in a 1925 movie, *Balto's Race to Nome*, and he also made appearances with silent screen star Mary Pickford. However, after the movie, the public lost interest and Balto ended up in a low-end circus sideshow, where he was cared for poorly. He was rescued by the children of Cleveland, Ohio, who heard of Balto's fate and organized a fund drive to save him. Thanks to the children of Cleveland, Balto was rescued from the side show and transported to the Cleveland Zoo, where he died in 1933. Balto was mounted and is on display at the Cleveland Museum of Natural History. A statue of Balto was unveiled in Manhattan's Central Park in 1925; the legend on the statue commemorates all of the brave dogs of the serum run.

Balto wasn't everyone's favorite! Leonard Seppala, a Norwegian and one of the better known mushers who ran the relay, resented the publicity given to "the movie dog," Balto, stating that it was actually Togo who served as lead dog during the most hazardous leg of the relay. Seppala bred dogs from the Chukchi Inuit stock and Togo was half Alaskan malamute. Togo died in Poland Spring, Maine, at the kennels of Elizabeth Ricker.

ON EXPLORATION

Seaman, the Newfoundland dog of Captain Meriwether Lewis, participated in Lewis and Clark's journey to the West. Lewis purchased his "dogg of the Newfoundland breed" for $20 (quite a price at the time). For years, historians knew the dog as Scannon, due to Lewis' poor handwriting in his frequent journal entries; however, closer analysis revealed the correct name, appropriate for a famous maritime breed. The incidents in Lewis's journals featuring Seaman give a picture of a dog who was a credit to his breed. Lewis was offered "three beverskins" for the dog by a Shawnee Indian but he declined to trade. In May 1805, Seaman was bitten by a beaver, lacerating an artery in his hind leg. Lewis and Clark performed surgery, and to Lewis's surprise (he had feared for Seaman's life), the dog recovered. Other entries tell of Seaman warning of bears, chasing marauding buffalo out of camp, and towing a deer wounded by gunshot out of the river (where it had fled) and into camp. Seaman's sufferings, from prickly grass seeds, mosquitoes, and heat, are also detailed. In 1806, Lewis named a Montana creek after Seaman (today the creek is known as Monture Creek).

Surprisingly, mention of Seaman diminishes in the journals, and his final fate is not known. However, in 1814, a writer named Timothy Allen wrote of seeing a dog collar in a museum in Alexandria, Virginia. He copied the inscription:

> "The greatest traveler of my species. My name is SEAMAN,
> the dog of Captain Meriwether Lewis, whom I accompanied to the
> Pacifick Ocean through the interior of the continent of North America."

In 1812, William Clark had donated items to a museum in Alexandria. However, the museum burned down, so the veracity of the collar cannot be verified.

BYRD'S DOG

Igloo, a fox terrier, belonged to Rear Admiral Richard Byrd and accompanied Byrd on the expeditions to the North and South Poles. Igloo had special protective clothing for the expeditions.

WAR HEROES

Sled dogs played a variety of roles on the battlefronts of World War I. During construction of the vital Washington–Alaska Military Cable and Telegraph System, sled dogs moved equipment and supplies so that work could continue during Alaska's winter cold. The type of dog used was often the "Mackenzie River husky," a catchall term for dogs bred in Alaska as freight huskies capable of pulling loads through deep snow. These dogs are taller, rangier, and longer coated than the AKC-type of husky or malamute. To keep the dogs from killing each other during fights, their incisors were pulled out or filed off, a practice used by the Inuit.

OFF TO WAR

During the winter of 1914–15 in World War I, sled dogs carried ammunition and supplies to French soldiers battling German troops in the Vosges Mountains. The dogs were transported from Alaska to France, traveling across the Atlantic, a tricky maneuver because the ocean was full of German submarines. The dogs were trained to be quiet during the passage so they wouldn't give away the position of their ship.

Once the dogs arrived, they delivered tons of ammunition and supplies to previously inaccessible regions. Three of these dogs were awarded the French Croix de Guerre.

Dog teams also supplied Italian troops fighting the Austro-Hungarian army on the Italian front, at altitudes up to 11,500 feet (3,500 m). They delivered ammunition and food in conditions far too harsh for horses or mules.

FILAX

In February 1917, Filax of Lewanno, a German shepherd, credited with rescuing 54 soldiers from the trenches of World War I, was exhibited as a hero at the Westminster Dog Show in Madison Square Garden.

STUBBY

In 1917, during World War I, a homeless, crossbred bulldog wandered into the encampment of the 102nd Yankee Infantry billeted at the Yale Bowl in New Haven, Connecticut. Wrapped in the overcoat of Corporal J. Robert Conroy and smuggled aboard a troop ship bound for the Western Front in France, Stubby participated in 17 battles and 4 offensives. He was wounded by a grenade in one attack, helped to detain—by the seat of the pants—a German spy (he wore the German's iron cross on his dog blanket for the rest of his days), and served as a vital lookout and companion to lonely sentries in foxholes. Despite his unauthorized entry into the war, after the Armistice, Stubby was personally decorated by General "Black Jack" Pershing. Stubby's 1926 *New York Times* obituary ran for half a page.

IN THE LINE OF DUTY

During the Battle of Guam in World War II, 25 Doberman pinschers were killed in action. Dr. William Putney, a veterinarian who commanded the Dobermans and their handlers during the battle, stated that they saved hundreds of lives. The dogs served as sentries and scouts and explored caves that the enemy used as hideouts. Many of the dogs had been donated by their families to serve as soldiers. "Dogs for Defense" was a 1942 campaign to persuade dog owners to donate "quality" dogs to the Army Quartermaster Corps. The war dog memorial, "Always Faithful," created by artist Susan Wilner, was unveiled at the Pentagon in July 1994. The memorial depicts Kurt, a Doberman scout on Guam who went ahead to reconnoiter a location and was bombarded by grenades. Kurt's death saved the men who followed him. Beneath Kurt's statue are engraved the names of the other Dobermans who lost their lives: Skipper, Ni, Miss, Blitz, Bursch, Yonnie, Poncho, Prince, Cappy, Arno, Pepper, Koko, Tubby, Fritz, Duke, Silver, Ludwig, Bunkie, Hobo, Emmy, Max, Brocky, and Ricky.

MORE WAR HEROES

BAMSE

His name might mean "teddy bear" in Norwegian, but Bamse the Saint Bernard was more than just a cuddly companion. Originally from Norway, Bamse journeyed to Scotland in 1940 with his master, Captain Erling Hafto.

Bamse was renowned as a brave member of the Norwegian Navy vessel *Thorodd*. In battle, he would stand in the ship's foremost gun turret, wearing a steel helmet specially made for him by his shipmates. He also rescued an officer from a knife-wielding attacker and jumped into the sea to rescue a man who fell overboard.

For most of World War II, *Thorodd* was stationed in Montrose and Dundee, and Bamse became a familiar figure in the local area. One of his duties was to round up his crewmates at the end of shore leave. Wearing a special bus pass on his collar, Bamse would scout around the local bars, sniffing out Norwegian sailors and escorting them back to base.

As a result of his bravery and intelligence, Bamse became the mascot of the Norwegian Navy and was famously photographed wearing a Norwegian sailor's cap. When he died of heart failure in 1944, Bamse was buried in Montrose with full military honors, his head facing the Norwegian home he would never see again. To this day, the Norwegian Navy holds a service of commemoration at his grave every ten years.

SMOKEY

When one thinks of a war dog, a 4-pound (1.8-kg) Yorkshire terrier is not the breed that comes to mind, but Smokey certainly qualifies. Found abandoned in a New Guinea foxhole by a soldier who didn't like dogs and purchased for $6.44 by William Wynne, a soldier who did aerial reconnaissance, Smokey accompanied Wynne on 12 aerial combat missions. Smokey also completed one mission that only a small dog could accomplish—pulling wires through a 8-inch (3-cm) wide, 70-foot (21-m) long culvert, enabling communications lines to be connected at a vital airfield. Were it not for Smokey's successfully completed mission, it would have been necessary to excavate the entire field in order to connect the lines. Smokey was also a vital therapy dog.

Constantly happy and extremely smart (Wynne spent his spare time in New Guinea training the little dog in obedience exercises and tricks), she visited many hospitalized troops. Smokey accompanied Wynne home from the war and died in 1957 at the age of 14.

JUDY

A purebred English pointer, Judy (1936–50) was the only dog registered as a Japanese POW during World War II. A ship's dog on a naval vessel, Judy repeatedly alerted the crew to the approach of Japanese war planes, long before the crew themselves could hear the planes' approach. When the ship was finally sunk in action, Judy became a registered POW, along with her shipmates, at an internment camp in Sumatra. Somehow, despite their own perilous state, the crew managed to convince the Japanese to call the dog a POW instead of killing her outright. During her two years as a POW, Judy was bitten by alligators and wounded by gunshot, but she survived. Her toughness and typical canine cheerfulness were a tremendous morale booster to her fellow prisoners. After the liberation of the camp in 1950, Judy returned to England with Frank Williams, a British airman and fellow POW. Judy was awarded the Dickin Medal.

NEMO

Trained as a sentry dog, Nemo was an 85-pound (38-kg) German shepherd and one of 4,000 dogs that served in Vietnam. One December night in 1966, Nemo and his handler, 22-year old Airman Robert Thorneburg, were assigned to patrol the perimeter of Tan Son Nhut airbase outside Saigon. It was a dangerous assignment because the base had been attacked the night before, and Viet Cong were presumed to be in the area. On the edge of an old Vietnamese cemetery, Thorneburg noticed his dog tense, then they were immediately attacked. Thorneburg was shot in the shoulder. A bullet entered just under Nemo's eye and exited his mouth; however, the dog continued to attack the Viet Cong, holding them off from his handler and giving Thorneburg time to radio for help. Nemo continued to guard Thorneburg even after more soldiers arrived. Eight more Viet Cong were discovered in the area; Nemo's actions had saved the base from another invasion. Veterinarians managed to save Nemo, but he lost his eye and was returned to the United States, one of the few dogs who served during Vietnam who actually returned alive. He spent the rest of his life as an honored resident of the sentry dog training school in Texas and died in 1973. He was buried with military honors.

DICKIN MEDAL WINNERS

The Dickin Medal is Great Britain's highest canine honor, awarded to animals for their work during wartime. It was established in 1943 by Maria Dickin, founder of the PDSA (People's Dispensary for Sick Animals). The recipient receives a bronze medallion with the words "For Gallantry" and "We Also Serve." Between 1943 and 1949, 18 dogs received the award—along with 3 horses, 1 cat, and 32 pigeons.

🐾 BOB, 1943: A white mongrel, he was the first dog to receive the Dickin Medal. He alerted an infantry battalion to the presence of the enemy, saving the entire battalion from surprise attack.

🐾 ROB, 1945: Took part in landings during the North African campaign with Infantry and later with the Special Air Unit in Italy.

🐾 SHEILA, 1945: This sheepdog helped to rescue four American airmen lost in a blizzard after an air crash in December 1944. Sheila was the first civilian dog to be awarded the Dickin Medal.

🐾 REX, 1945: A civilian rescue dog, awarded the medal "for outstanding good work in the location of casualties in burning buildings."

Undaunted by smouldering debris, thick smoke, intense heat, and jets of water from fire hoses, this dog displayed uncanny intelligence and outstanding determination in his efforts to follow up a scent that led him to a casualty.

🐾 BEAUTY, 1945: Led the Animal Rescue Squads during the bombing of London in World War II. Beauty, a wire-haired terrier, received the Pioneer Medal (usually reserved for humans) from the PDSA for all the lives she saved. She also received a silver mounted collar inscribed, "For Services Rendered."

🐾 JET, 1945: A civilian dog who helped to rescue people trapped under bombed buildings during the Blitz (when the Germans heavily bombed London in World War II).

IRMA, 1945: Also a civilian dog, she rescued Londoners trapped under bombed buildings during the Blitz.

ANTIS, 1949: A German shepherd, served with his Czech owner in the French Air Force and RAF from 1940 to 1945 in both North Africa and England. He is the first non-English dog to receive the Dickin Medal.

THORN, 1945: Located air raid casualties in spite of thick smoke in burning buildings.

TICH, 1949: This mongrel bitch showed "loyalty, courage, and devotion to duty under hazardous conditions of war from 1941 to 1945, while serving in North Africa and Italy."

GANDER, 2000: He is the only canine from Canada to receive the Dickin Medal. Gander was a Newfoundland who saved Canadian infantrymen in the battle of Lye Mun on Hong Kong in December 1941.

RIFLEMAN KHAN, 1945: At the Battle of Walcheren, November 1944, the dog rescued Lt. Cpl. Muldoon from drowning while under heavy shell fire.

RIP, 1940: A mongrel dog who located many air raid victims buried by rubble during the Blitz.

PETER, 1946: A collie dog who located victims trapped under bombed buildings during the Blitz.

PUNCH AND JUDY, 1946: A boxer dog and bitch, recognized for saving the lives of two British Officers in Israel by attacking an armed terrorist; during the attack, Punch was shot and Judy's back was grazed by bullets.

RICKY, 1947: A Welsh sheepdog who helped clear mines from a canal bank in Holland. When one of the mines exploded, Ricky was wounded but kept working.

BRIAN, 1947: A German shepherd patrol dog of a parachute battalion, he landed in Normandy; after doing the required number of jumps, he became a fully qualified paratrooper.

OFFICIAL DOGS

MS. MAYOR

Shanda, a golden retriever, was elected mayor of Guffey, Colorado, from 1993–98. Shanda's Repuppkin party was said to have easily defeated the rival Democats. Shanda's spokesperson stated that her platform was based on abolishing all leash laws.

OFFICIAL STATE DOGS

It is shocking that so few states have been enterprising and forward thinking enough to designate official state dogs, but here is the list of enlightened states to date:

STATE	TYPE OF DOG	YEAR OF DESIGNATION
Louisiana	Catahoula leopard dog	1979
Maryland	Chesapeake bay retriever	1964
Massachusetts	Boston terrier	1979
North Carolina	Plott hound	1989
Pennsylvania	Great Dane	1965
South Carolina	Boykin spaniel	1985
Virginia	American foxhound	1966
Wisconsin	American water spaniel	1985

CATAHOULA LEOPARD DOGS

The official state dog of Louisiana, Catahoulas have "cracked glass" or "marbled" eyes, which can be any of a variety of spooky combinations of blue-white, half blue and half green, white, gray, or amber. The eyes of Catahoulas are similar to collectible, stippled marbles and "cracked glass" eyes are highly prized in the breed. Catahoulas are also known for their ability to climb trees.

SOME INQUISITIVE DOGS

 DOGGIE DISCOVERY

One of the most exciting archaeological sites of the twentieth century—the Lascaux Cave—was supposedly found by a dog. On September 12, 1940, near the town of Montignac in France, 17-year-old Marcel Ravidat was out walking his dog, Robot, with three friends when Robot disappeared. The teenagers searched high and low, and eventually found that Robot had fallen into a strange hole. Upon further investigation, it turned out that the hole was the entrance to a cavern decorated with some of the most incredible prehistoric wall paintings ever discovered. The cave is now a UNESCO World Heritage Site, and is preserved for future generations—all thanks to Robot!

 DAISY THE DACHSUND

A miniature wire-haired dachshund called Daisy bit off more than she could chew in 2007 when she unearthed a fossilized bone on a beach in Suffolk. The 13-inch (33-cm) bone, believed to come from a mammoth, weighed in at 8 pounds (3.6 kg)—nearly as much as Daisy herself. It was found after a violent storm scoured away sand from the beach, revealing the bone, which was estimated to be 2 million years old. Unfortunately for Daisy, her ancient find wasn't edible. She had to settle for the leg bone from her owner's roast lamb.

 TRAINING REGIME

Staffordshire bull terrier Bud went walkies in a big way in 2004 when he made a remarkable journey from his home in Darlington, England—by train. The commuting canine first scaled a 7-foot (2.1-m)-high garden fence, then crossed a park and a busy road before reaching the local train station and boarding a 6:00 a.m. train bound for London. However, perhaps the bright lights of the big city didn't appeal, because Bud disembarked in York, a mere 60 miles (96.5 km) from home. Luckily, train employees saw Bud wandering around York station and summoned his owner to come and pick him up.

CHAPTER 6

Always at our Side

Sometimes it seems as though our dogs know our true

selves. Always at our side, both earthy and yet spiritual

companions, they see and accept us as we are. This

mystical bond sometimes has life-saving practical

applications, such as when dogs step in to warn of seizures

or cancer—a skill that medical science has yet to explain.

CANINE MASCOTS

SMOKEY, BLUETICK COONHOUND, UNIVERSITY OF TENNESSEE: The bluetick breed originated in Tennessee. There have been eight Smokeys since 1953. The Smokeys have had various trials. One was kidnapped by University of Kentucky students; one Smokey had a brief on-field altercation with the Baylor University mascot, a bear (after all, the bluetick is a hunting hound); in 1991, one almost expired from post-game heat exhaustion; and one Smokey had a vendetta against a tuba player in the band, whom he tried to bite on several occasions. All of the Smokeys have their day-to-day activities supervised by the Alpha Gamma Rho fraternity, who consider it an honor to handle Smokey.

UGA, WHITE BULLDOG, UNIVERSITY OF GEORGIA: Named by *Sports Illustrated* as the number one U.S. mascot, Uga has made the cover of the magazine three times. Ugas I, II, III, IV, and V repose in eternal rest in marble vaults near the main gate of the University of Georgia's Sanford Stadium.

BULLY, BULLDOG, MISSISSIPPI STATE: In 1939, the first Bully was hit by a bus. He was honored by a solemn funeral procession at the college, and his coffin lay in state.

HANDSOME DAN, BULLDOG, YALE UNIVERSITY: First mascot ever adopted by a college, in 1889. Handsome Dan I was purchased from a local blacksmith for $5 in 1889. Handsome Dan II, somewhat of a traitor, was kidnapped by Harvard students, who circulated upsetting pictures of a contented Dan II settling in at Harvard. Handsome Dan III retired early—he didn't like the rowdy crowds at the games.

REVEILLE, COLLIE, TEXAS A&M UNIVERSITY: The first two Reveilles were a mutt and a German shepherd. Since then, all the Reveilles have been purebred collies. After death, the Reveilles are buried in a special cemetery on the outskirts of the field, and a small scoreboard oriented toward this cemetery so that the Reveilles—even in death—can exert a positive influence on the score.

🐾 SPIRIT, ALASKAN MALAMUTE, UNIVERSITY OF WASHINGTON: The husky was selected as the school mascot by student committee in 1922. A costumed "Harry the Husky" performs at sporting and special events, and a live Alaskan malamute, currently named Spirit, has traditionally led the UW football team onto the field at the start of games. Unfortunately, huskies and malamutes are not the same thing, as any devotee of either breed will be anxious to tell you.

🐾 JONATHAN, HUSKY, UNIVERSITY OF CONNECTICUT: The University of Connecticut is popularly known as "UConn" (pronounced Yukon), hence the husky mascot designated in 1933. Students named the husky "Jonathan" for Jonathan Trumbull, Connecticut's first governor. The current Jonathan is the twelfth husky. An on-campus husky statue was dedicated in 1995—students rub the nose for good luck.

🐾 SALUKI, SOUTHERN ILLINOIS UNIVERSITY: Salukis are swift-running sighthounds domesticated in Egypt at least 4,000 years ago. The area of Illinois where SIU is located was known as "Little Egypt" because it was a productive grain-producing region even during drought, just as Egypt was for Joseph in the Bible— hence, the Saluki.

🐾 SCOTTISH TERRIER, CARNEGIE MELLON UNIVERSITY: Carnegie Mellon is named after steel baron Andrew Carnegie, who was a native Scot.

🐾 BULLDOG, THE MARINE CORPS: The first mascot was a bulldog named Jiggs, whelped in 1922 and registered as "King Bulwark." Unfortunately, Jiggs/King Bulwark died in 1927 before the age of 5. He lay in state at marine headquarters in Quantico, VA, flanked by a Marine honor guard. Succeeding generations of Marine bulldog mascots have all been named "Chesty."

MEDICAL ALERT

CANCER DETECTORS

We all know that dogs are man's best friend, but until relatively recently even scientists didn't realize that a dog could actually save your life by detecting cancer. In 1978, Gillian Lacey believed she was completely fit and healthy. However, Trudii, her beloved dalmatian, thought otherwise. Gillian noticed that Trudii was always sniffing at a freckle on her leg, and although Gillian couldn't see anything unusual, she decided to visit her physician. When the "freckle" was removed, tests revealed it was a malignant melanoma, a type of cancer that is better to treat as soon as possible.

Of course, it's possible to regard Trudii's diagnosis as a fluke. However, dog owner Hazel Woodget is firmly convinced that her dog, a Chihuahua named Pepe, saved her life not just once, but three times. Pepe first began behaving oddly by nuzzling against Hazel's left breast. Within a week, Hazel had been diagnosed with breast cancer and later had to undergo a mastectomy. Doctors remarked that the cancer was already well advanced and, had it gone unnoticed for much longer, it would probably have become terminal.

For several months, Pepe's behavior returned to normal; however, around Christmas he again began to act strangely. Fearing the worst, Hazel returned to her physician. Tests revealed that Hazel's cancer had indeed returned and she needed further surgery. Incredibly, this wasn't the end of the story. Another six months later, Pepe's peculiar behavior returned once again. The cancer had spread to Hazel's right breast, and a third operation was required to remove it.

Scientists believe that dogs like Pepe and Trudii are somehow able to sniff out the presence of cancerous cells. Research is now under way to discover exactly how these animals can do it, in the hope that more lives can be saved.

SEIZURE PREDICTOR

One of the worst aspects of epilepsy is that people with the condition cannot predict when a seizure may strike. However, there is increasing evidence that dogs can do just that. Some medical centers now provide "seizure alert dogs."

Tony Brown-Griffin used to have more than a dozen epileptic seizures in a single week. The condition prevented her from leaving her home or enjoying socializing with friends. Now, with the help of golden retriever Ajay, she lives an almost entirely normal life. About 40 minutes before a seizure, Ajay gives Tony a warning lick on the hand, giving her plenty of time to get herself to a safe place. The peace of mind that Ajay provides has an added benefit for Tony—the reduction in stress and worry means that she now has fewer seizures, just a couple each week.

Ajay can predict Tony's seizures with 100 percent accuracy, although no one knows precisely how. However, scientists believe that Ajay may be picking up on subtle changes in smell caused by increased sweating. What is certain is that Ajay and other dogs like him are giving people with epilepsy a new lease on life.

DIABETIC FORECASTER

Belle the beagle is owned by Kevin Weaver, a diabetic living in Ocoee, Florida. The canine had been trained to detect potential diabetic attacks by licking and sniffing his owner's nose. In this way, he can check Kevin's blood sugar levels. When Kevin became unconscious, Belle called an ambulance crew by biting on her owner's cell phone. The dog used her teeth to press a key programmed to call the emergency services. When the phone call was answered, only barking was heard on the line, but an ambulance crew (aware that Belle is an alert dog) rushed to the house.

HEROIC CANINES

 SHELBY

A seven-year-old German shepherd from Ely, Iowa, Shelby saved the lives of two adults and two children—who were overnight guests—when she alerted them to dangerously high carbon monoxide levels in the house. Janet Walderbach had passed out because of the fumes, but Shelby nudged her until Janet woke up. Shelby then woke up John Walderbach. She acted anxious and would not leave their sides. John thought Shelby needed a trip outdoors, but when he put her outside, she began to bark, whine, and scratch at the door continuously until John, Janet, and the children were safely outside. The four people were treated for carbon monoxide poisoning at a hospital. Doctors informed them that they were lucky to escape long-term damage, even death.

 COPPER

In February 2000, Copper, a three-legged golden retriever, saved his family, the Camerons (four people, two cats, and a parrot) from an electrical fire that destroyed the Cameron's Raleigh, North Carolina, home. Christy Cameron, deep in sleep, awoke to Copper's persistent pawing. The house was in flames, but Copper's alert allowed everyone to escape.

 SPIKE

A two-year-old American pitbull terrier named Spike saved his owner Dr. Danny Fredman of Tucson, Arizona, in 2007, when he was about to dive into his pool. Spike began barking incessantly, and when Danny turned on the pool lights to investigate, he found a 5-foot (1.5-m) western diamondback rattlesnake coiled up on the surface of the water.

 SAM

David Biddle was attending Lehigh University in Bethlehem, Pennsylvania. One morning, Sam, a black Labrador-rottweiler mix owned by David, began scratching and whining at a door to wake up his roommates. They found David with a 108°F (42°C) fever. He was taken to the hospital, and remained there for just over three months while he was treated for meningococcal meningitis. David survived because of Sam's diligence in waking up his roomates.

BRUTIS

In Pasco county in Florida, a golden retriever named Brutis came to the rescue of a grandmother and her two young grandchildren, who were playing outdoors, when he captured a snake. The alert dog had saved the children from a possible bite from a coral snake, one of the deadliest snakes in the world. Brutis wasn't so fortunate. When his owners, the Oretos, realized he had been bitten, he was rushed to a veterinarian. Luckily, after phone calls to several hospitals in the region, enough antivenom was found to treat the dog.

TOBY

Debbie Parkhurst of Maryland was taking a break from making jewelery and bit into an apple. However, suddenly she couldn't breathe and began to panic. A piece of apple was choking her.Toby, a golden retriever who had been rescued from a garbage can as a puppy, leaped upon her owner—something that she was not in the habit of doing. The piece of apple was dislodged and Debbie regained her breath.

JESSIE

Because Jamie Hanson of Wisconsin had an amputated leg, she had a specially trained golden retriever-shepherd mix to help her. In 2006, Jamie's cat had jumped onto a table and knocked over a lit candle, starting a fire. The heroic 13-year-old dog grabbed Jamie by her pajamas and pulled her to safety. The dog also brought the woman her prosthetic leg and a phone. As Jamie called for help, the brave dog raced back into the house to retrieve the cat. Tragically, cat and dog did not survive the fire.

LOYAL FRIENDS

GREYFRIARS BOBBY

One of the most famous dogs in history, Greyfriars Bobby was a Skye terrier who lived in Edinburgh, Scotland, in the nineteenth century with his owner, night watchman John Gray. The pair worked together every night for two years, and became inseparable. Then, in 1858, Gray died of tuberculosis. The loyal Bobby, however, did not forget his master. Local legend says that on the very night of Gray's burial, Bobby appeared at his grave in Greyfriars Kirkyard in Edinburgh's Old Town. Despite being chased away by the custodian of the graveyard, Bobby always returned. As his fame spread, crowds would gather at Greyfriars at 1:00 p.m. each day to watch Bobby emerge from the graveyard and trot down to the coffee house where his master had always dined. There, he was given a free meal. Bobby maintained his vigil at the graveside for 14 years until he himself died in 1872. Although Bobby could not be buried within consecrated ground, he was laid to rest just inside the gate of Greyfriars Kirkyard, near the grave of the master he had served loyally for so long.

KEEPING VIGIL

Attachment (1829) is a painting by Sir Edwin Henry Landseer. The painting is of a terrier who watched over his master, Charles Gough, for three months after Gough fell while mountain climbing in Scotland. Three months after Gough was reported missing, local highlanders heard a barking dog and discovered the dog keeping vigil. This story was also retold by Sir Walter Scott (*Helvellyn*) and the famous English Romantic poet William Wordsworth (*Fidelity*).

HACHIKO

Sometimes known as "the Japanese Greyfriars Bobby," Hachiko was a rare Akita who belonged to Professor Hidesamuroh Ueno. Every evening, Hachiko would wait at Tokyo's Shibuya Station for his master to return from his work at the city's university. However, one day in 1925 Professor Ueno never arrived. He had died at his office. Undeterred, Hachiko continued to turn up at the station at the same time each evening, waiting hopefully for his owner. Regular commuters who knew his sad story christened him *chuken* Hachiko ("the faithful little dog" Hachiko). In 1934, a bronze statue of the Akita was unveiled at the station, with Hachiko present as guest of honor. Hachiko finally died in 1935, but he remains an enormously popular figure in Japan—so much so that his life has been turned into a movie starring Richard Gere in *Hachiko: A Dog's Story* (2008).

DOGS AT WORK—YOURS, NOT THEIRS!

The traditional American view of dogs as strictly verboten in the workplace is slowly changing, particularly in the case of small businesses in high-growth industries, such as software companies, that compete for the best employees and try hard to keep them happy. June 22, 2007, was Take Your Dog To Work Day in the United States (sponsored by Pet Sitters International). If you'd like to encourage this trend, here are some hints for making sure that dogs and workplace productivity are not mutually incompatible:

- 🐾 Exercise the dog thoroughly before you bring him to work.
- 🐾 Bring some chew toys to occupy the dog.
- 🐾 A dog that goes to work should be presocialized to strangers and other dogs.
- 🐾 The dog should be housebroken and parasite-free.
- 🐾 Clean up after your dog outside the workplace!
- 🐾 Keep dangerous cords, important reports, etc. away from the dog.
- 🐾 Bring a dogbed so that your dog has its own "place" inside your office or cubicle.

IN MEMORY

PUBLIC PET CEMETERY

Located just outside Paris on a forested islet in the suburb of Asnières sur Seine, the Cimitière des Chiens (see page 97) is the world's oldest public pet cemetery. The cemetery was a result of an 1898 Paris law that decreed that dead pets could no longer be disposed of in the garbage. Attorney Georges Harmois and journalist Marguerite Durand came up with the idea of a cemetery for dogs and other domestic animals (but it is known as the Cimitière des Chiens, or "Cemetery of Dogs"). Opened in summer 1899, on riverfront land, the cemetery boasts an elegant Art Nouveau gateway, elaborate monuments, and ornate tombstones. No crosses are permitted on the graves. Before burial, the coffin has to be opened to verify that it contains an animal. At least 40,000 animals have been buried there.

PRIVATE CEMETERY

The Canine Cemetery in Hartsdale, New York, founded in 1896 by New York City veterinarian Samuel Johnson, is the world's oldest private pet cemetery. Over 70,000 pets are buried at Hartsdale, including those of Joe Garagiola, Kate Smith, Elizabeth Arden, MacKinlay Kantor (author of *The Voice Legend of Bugle Ann*), and Louise Lasser.

BEYOND CREMATION

For a truly eternal remembrance of your favorite dog, you can turn his ashes into a diamond ring. Some dog lovers have done just that, such as one dog lover who had the ashes of her two dogs (and her cat) turned into a 6-carat diamond ring. The ashes were sent to Life Gem UK, which will make diamonds from pet—and human—ashes. Carbon from the ashes is heated to 5,430°F (3,000°C) and various chemicals are added. In about two weeks, a rough diamond is formed. No word on whether dog and diamond lover Elizabeth Taylor ever took advantage of this service.

SIRIUS, THE ONLY DOG TO DIE

At least 300 search and rescue dogs from all over the country, along with 50 FEMA-certified rescue dogs and the New York City Canine Corps, assisted rescue workers in the weeks after the World Trade Center and Pentagon tragedies that occurred on September 11, 2001. Surprisingly, only one dog is known to have died as a direct result of these horrendous attacks.

Sirius, a yellow Labrador, was a trained bomb-detection dog employed by the Port Authority police to search and clear commercial vehicles before they could enter the Trade Center's underground garage. On that fateful morning, when Sirius' human handler, police officer David Lim, realized something was wrong, he kenneled Sirius in the police department's underground headquarters and told the dog "You stay there . . . I'll be back for you." Lim rushed upstairs to see how he could help, but in minutes the towers collapsed, trapping both Lim and Sirius. Lim was rescued, but Sirius did not survive.

Sirius' remains were later recovered from the kennel site, along with his dog bowl, which was returned to an emotional Lim. Lim treasures a photograph of himself and his hard-working dog taken at Windows on the World—the famous restaurant that was at the very top of the trade center—in the year before the tragedy. Sirius was buried at the Canine Cemetery in Hartsdale (see opposite).

FAMOUS DOG EPITAPHS

> *"Near this spot are deposited the remains of one who possessed*
> *Beauty without Vanity, Strength without Insolence,*
> *Courage without Ferocity, and all the Virtues of Man,*
> *Without his vices.*
> *This praise, which would be unmeaning flattery if*
> *inscribed over human ashes, is but*
> *A just tribute to the memory of Boatswain, a dog."*
>
> TRIBUTE TO THE MEMORY OF BOATSWAIN, A DOG
> LORD BYRON (1788–1824)
>
>
>
> *"His friends he loved—his fellest foes—cats—I believe he did but feign to hate.*
> *Mine hand will miss the insinuated nose,*
> *Mine eyes the tail that wagged contempt at fate."*
>
> EPITAPH FOR A DOG
> SIR WILLIAM WATSON (1858–1935)

MEMOIRS OF DOGS

This genre, written by devoted owners, is extensive enough to warrant a graduate school literature seminar!

Angus: A Memoir, Charles Siebert
My Dog Tulip, J. R. Ackerley
Marley and Me, John Grogan
Bob: The True Story of an English Springer Spaniel, Blanche Shoemaker Wagstaff
Colter: The True Story of the Best Dog I Ever Had, Rick Bass
My Dog Skip, Willie Morris
Travels With Lisbeth, Lars Eighner (homeless man and his dog)
Clara, the Early Years, Margot Kaufman
Travels With Charlie, John Steinbeck
Every Night, Josephine, Jacqueline Susann
Mostly Bob, Tom Corwin
A Good Dog: The Story of Orson, Who Changed My Life, Jon Katz
Dog Years: A Memoir, Mark Doty

CANINE BENEFACTORS

At the end of the 1990s, only a few states recognized pet "trusts." Nowadays, all 50 states and Washington, D.C. have laws validating legally drawn up pet trusts. However, because the law traditionally views animals as property, property cannot be left property. Realistically, it is usually best to choose a trusted guardian for the dog, make your wishes known in your will, and leave the money in trust to the guardian.

🐾 In 1992, German shepherds Gunther III and Gunther IV were left $124 million by Countess Karlotta Liebenstein. In 2000, Madonna sold her Miami estate for $7.5 million to agents acting for Gunther IV.

🐾 In 2007, Leona Helmsley left $12 million to her Yorkie, Trouble. Trouble will stay with Ms. Helmsley's brother, Alvin Rosenthal. The will orders the cash to be put into a special trust to benefit the dog, and a trustee will be named to make sure the money is spent as Helmsley wanted, which probably includes a security detail (of pitbulls and rottweilers?) and dog walkers (degreed veterinarians?), as well as gourmet eats (Zabar's on call!!)

🐾 Drew Barrymore deeded her 3,600 square foot (334.5 sq m) home to her Labrador Flossie after Flossie saved Drew from a house fire.

🐾 Tina and Kate, collie crosses, were left £450,000 each and the run of an estate (complete with caretaker) near Bath, England.

🐾 In 1995, a Labrador cross called Jasper enjoyed a remarkable reversal of fortunes. After being abandoned by his owner, Jasper ended up in London's Battersea Dogs Home. The poor dog was destined to be put to sleep, when he was granted a last-minute reprieve and was adopted by Diana Myburgh, a wealthy heiress. As Jasper settled into his new home, alongside Diana's other dog, Jason, there was another twist in Jasper's fate. Just months later, his new owner died, leaving each of her two pets a £25,000 legacy. Since the original inheritance, Jasper's bequest has been tripled—thanks to the investments of his guardian, Sir Benjamin Slade, who is Ms. Myburgh's son-in-law.

CHAPTER 7

Caring for a Dog

In the old days, dogs often lived in the barn or outside,

tethered to a doghouse, and fed leftovers. They were

allowed to wander the neighborhood without supervision.

Today's standards of dog care are far higher. Our dogs

share our homes, eat specially prepared dog food, and

any dog wandering freely would probably be apprehended

by the authorities. Unfortunately, today's busy lives also

mean that our dogs are often left alone and become bored.

This chapter contains some hints to keep the modern dog

healthy, safe, and occupied.

GETTING A DOG: SOME THINGS TO THINK ABOUT

Sometimes it just happens. A dog finds you, or you buy or adopt a dog on a whim. But remember that a dog isn't just for Christmas. Before taking in a dog, make sure you're prepared to make a huge investment in time—and money. Dogs need plenty of attention and exercise. Vet bills can be expensive, and so can feeding a dog, especially a large breed.

SHELTERS

You can consider adopting a homeless dog. Homeless dogs can be purebred as well as mixed breeds. More than 12 million dogs are euthanized in shelters each year, and 25 percent of these are purebreds. If you have your heart set on a certain breed, look into the "Rescue" groups for that breed, which can be easily found on the Internet. You'll find a dog in the breed you want, but with the satisfaction of knowing you've given a home to the homeless. If you are not set on a purebred, most of the larger Animal Welfare or Rescue Organizations today run very fine shelters. They vaccinate and neuter the dogs in their care and some will provide much costlier, necessary veterinarian care before they will offer a dog for adoption. Good shelters will assess the personality of a particular dog and advise you of a dog that suits your own home situation. Shelters can be picky about who they will allow to adopt a dog, and the adoption, often, is not free. Adoption fees for shelter dogs can run up to several hundred dollars, but realize that this is not profit—the money you pay goes to run the shelter and care for more homeless dogs.

BREEDERS

If you want a dog of championship pedigree, your best bet is a private breeder rather than a pet store. Pet store puppies may look cute, and the store may look clean, but that puppy probably came from a commercial breeder and may not have had the best start in life. If you buy from a private breeder, you will be able to meet the breeder and the mother and see how the dogs are kept.

🐾 Conscientious breeders are knowledgeable about the health issues in their breed and are willing to discuss them. They have done genetic testing and pedigree analysis to try to ensure that their puppies will be free of genetic diseases that are common in pedigree dogs. They can provide documented evidence of this pedigree analysis and genetic testing, such as a certificate from the Orthopedic Foundation for Animals (OFA) evaluating the hip joints of the litter's sire and dam, or certification from the Canine Eye Registration Foundation (CERF) that the litter's sire and dam have tested free of heritable eye disease.

🐾 They are willing for you to meet their dogs. They are proud of their dogs, and when you meet the dogs, you understand why they would be proud.

🐾 They will carefully assess your ability to care for the dog. They will request and check references, may ask to visit your home, and will frequently ask you to sign a legal contract stating that if you no longer want the dog, you will return it to the breeder. Good breeders are interested in the fate of the dogs they breed for the life of the dog. They take responsibility. They do not take your money, hand you a puppy, and close the door on the transaction forever.

PUPPY BROKERS

🐾 "Licensed Breeder" means that the breeder of the dog must be registered with the USDA. The USDA requires large-scale dog breeders to be registered.

🐾 The USDA requires that the size of a dog's living cage must be only 6 inches (15 cm) longer than the dog from tip of the nose to base of the tail. Is this the way you'd like to see your pet treated?

COMMON GENETIC
DISEASES

Dogs, especially purebreds, are subject to a wide variety of genetic diseases. If you are interested in a breed, find out what diseases it is prone to, and ask to see proof of genetic testing done on the puppy's parents! It is often possible to have both parents tested and certified as free of a particular disease, or to have a pedigree analyzed for disease carriers. Good breeders should do this type of testing and pedigree analysis, and they should be willing to discuss it. The following diseases are just a few of the more common genetic problems:

AORTIC STENOSIS: Narrowed aorta causes changes in the electrical rhythm of the heart, leading to sudden death. Newfoundlands and golden retrievers.

ATOPIC DERMATITIS: Common skin disease linked to inhalant allergies.

GENETIC PREDISPOSITION TO CANCERS: About 80 percent of deaths in flat-coated retrievers are caused by cancer, especially hemangiosarcoma; it is thought to be the result of a defect on the p53 gene, which suppresses tumors.

CHERRY EYE: Prolapsed tear gland, giving the dog a red-eyed appearance and making the eyes susceptible to infection. Cocker spaniels, beagles, and bloodhounds.

DEAFNESS: More common in white breeds. About 30 percent of dalmatians are deaf in one or both ears. Other breeds with a high incidence are English setters, bull terriers, and Australian cattle dogs.

GASTRIC DILATATION-VOLVULUS:
Large, deep-chested breeds, such as the bloodhound, Great Dane, and Gordon setter are more likely to experience "bloat." There is a genetic predisposition as well as conformational predisposition to this acute condition. It is a medical emergency that kills rapidly if not treated.

HIP DYSPLASIA:
Painful developmental malformation or subluxation of the hip joints that leads to painful and crippling arthritis. Very common!

HYPOTHYROIDISM: Common endocrine disorder. Autoimmune destruction of the thyroid affects more than 50 breeds.

PROGRESSIVE RETINAL ATROPHY:
Progressive degeneration of the retina in both eyes, leading to blindness. Many breeds are subject.

RUPTURED DISK: When damage occurs to one or more of the intervertebral disks in the spinal cord. This problem often occurs in dogs with short legs, but dachshunds are particularly at risk because they have such a long body.

VON WILLEBRANDS' DISEASE:
Bleeding disorder caused by defective blood platelet function; 59 breeds show some disposition to this disease, and it is most common in Doberman pinschers.

WOBBLER SYNDROME: Weakness starts in the hind legs and progresses to paralysis. Caused by abnormal neck vertebrae that compress the spinal cord. Great Danes and Dobermans.

BASIC DOGGY EQUIPMENT

I f you are acquiring a dog for the first time, there are a few basic essentials that you will need. These include:

- food and water bowls
- a bed or blanket to sleep on
- toys for play
- brushes (especially for long-haired breeds) to keep dog fur tidy
- toothpaste and brush specifically designed for dogs, not for humans—most dogs don't like the foaming action of human toothpastes
- dog chews (to prevent plaque buildup on teeth)
- a leash (especially if you walk your dog in urban areas with busy streets)
- a collar with identity tag

FOR THE GERIATRIC CANINE
An older dog with stiff joints is less comfortable sleeping curled up in a traditional dog bed and will prefer to stretch out instead. A beanbag makes a great bed—there are various designs available for dogs in different sizes. Also consider safety gates—the type you use for toddlers—to keep geriatric dogs from clambering up, then tumbling down stairs.

CLEAN TEETH
Brushing your dog's teeth will help prevent painful gums and tooth decay. Even an older dog can be trained to allow its teeth to be brushed. At first, lift the dog's upper lip and rub a piece of gauze in a circular motion on its teeth and gums. Once you've gained the dog's trust, add some toothpaste—remember, use only dog toothpaste—to the gauze; then use toothpaste on a brush. You can dip the gauze in some beef bouillon if the dog won't let you near its teeth at first.

COLLARED!

Of course, a dog collar is practical for restraining a dog and for carrying an identification tag to identify the dog if it gets lost, but for centuries dog collars protected the dog as well as established the wealth of the dog's owner. Fifteenth-, sixteenth-, and seventeenth-century iron dog collars featured fearsome spikes, intended to protect the throats of hunting hounds from wolves, bears, and wild boars. Austrian Baroque collars of the seventeenth and eighteenth centuries were made of leather decorated with ornate metalwork and lined with velvet. Early twentieth-century German collars have heavy leather inside and ornamental brass plates, engraved with dogs' heads, on the outside.

THE MICROCHIP, A LOST DOG'S BEST FRIEND

Microchips are small electronic devices about the size of a grain of rice that are coded with a unique identification number readable by a scanner. Microchips are implanted in a dog's skin between the shoulder blades via a sterile needle (the process is no more painful than a routine vaccine). To ensure that the body does not reject the microchip, they are encased in the same type of biocompatible glass used in human pacemakers. If a lost dog is found to be microchipped, veterinarians or animal welfare organizations can contact the national database that stores microchip numbers and the contact information of the microchipped dog's owner. Microchipping is a very good idea if you plan to take your dog along on a vacation to another part of the country. Dogs are particularly susceptible to becoming lost at unsettled times like these, and owners may not be familiar enough with the locality they lost their dog in to mount an effective search. Microchips give a lost dog the best chance of being reunited with its family.

THE HISTORY OF DOG FOOD

A popular early feeding method was "trencher feeding." A trencher was a long flat loaf of bread used as a plate. People would eat their meal from a trencher, then the bread, soaked by leftovers, and any remaining bones, would be tossed to the dogs.

The first processed dog food was the brainchild of an Ohio electrician named James Spratt, who in 1860 was in London selling lightning rods when he noticed packs of stray dogs swarming the London docks to eat the discarded, moldy hard tack thrown off the ships by sailors. Spratt concocted a biscuit of wheat, beets, vegetables, and beef blood that was marketed as Spratt's Patent Meat Fibrine Dog Cakes. Spratt's dog biscuit came in a tin decorated with terriers, and the legend "My Faithful Friend's Own Biscuit Box." Prior to Spratt's Fibrine Dog Cakes, dogs made do with whatever they could scrounge or their owners deigned to feed them.

In 1907, F. H. Bennett introduced "Milk Bone" dog biscuits as a "complete food." Spratt's Patent Fibrine Dog Cakes and Milk Bone biscuits were the big guns in the dog food game until the 1920s. At that time, many horses were unwanted, replaced by early automobiles, and Ken-L Ration introduced canned horse meat as a dog food. World War I put a serious crimp in Ken-L Ration's canned horse meat biz, because there was a shortage of tin for the cans.

Dry dog food was introduced in 1946, and in 1957 Purina perfected the extrusion method of manufacture. Most dog owners today have little memory of dog food before Purina Dog "Chow." In the 1960s, the industry began a concerted campaign, through the so-called "Pet Food Institute," via newspaper articles, women's magazines, and other media to convince dog owners that dogs should be fed dog food. Period. Dog owners were taught that dog feeding was too complex, that home-cooked meals would be mysteriously "missing essential nutrients." Go ahead, feed your baby, if you must, with whatever "balanced" swill you might concoct, but for Dog's sake, feed him ONLY DOG FOOD. This era saw the introduction of dog foods that "made their own gravy (just add water)!," "yummies," and cute little bones that came in attractive colors. No surprise that on the human food front, colorful and sugary cereals for children were also making inroads.

HUMAN FOODS THAT CAN POISON DOGS

🐾 CHOCOLATE: Due to a chemical compound, theobromine; the most poisonous type of chocolate is baking chocolate. Not all dogs are susceptible.

🐾 COFFEE: Caffeine causes tremor, agitation, or cardiac arrhythmia in some dogs.

🐾 GARLIC, including garlic powder. (Garlic until recently was marketed as a "natural" flea deterrent for dogs; that product line has recently disappeared.)

🐾 ONIONS AND ONION POWDER: A chemical compound, thiosulfate, can cause hemolytic anemia—all forms of onion or garlic can be problematic, including dehydrated onion and onions on leftover pizza.

🐾 MACADAMIA NUTS: Dogs eating the nuts have developed wobbly walking (ataxia), tremor, swollen limbs, and increased heart rate.

🐾 BREAD DOUGH: The yeast reacts to the stomach's warm, moist environment and expands, leading to stomach distention; it also forms ethanol, which is absorbed into the bloodstream and renders the dog's blood dangerously acidic.

🐾 AVOCADO: Contain a chemical called persin that can cause vomiting, diarrhea, edema (fluid accumulation), and cardiac muscle damage.

🐾 GRAPES AND RAISINS: These can cause irreversible kidney failure in dogs.

WHAT CORPORATION FEEDS YOUR DOG?

CORPORATION	BRAND
Nestle	Alpo, Mighty Dog, Purina One
Big Heart Pet Brands	Gravy Train, Kibbles-n-Bits, Nature's Recipe
Colgate-Palmolive	Hill's Science Diet
Mars	Eukanuba, Iams, Kal Kan, Pedigree

OUTDOOR MATTERS

THREE TRADITIONAL DESKUNKING REMEDIES

TOMATO JUICE

This remedy is so storied, one has to give it a certain amount of respect. However, most "survivors" of skunk attack agree that tomato juice merely removes the most pungent edge and makes your dog look like it survived an attack by a pot of marinara sauce.

MASSENGILL DOUCHE

Two ounces (57 g) of Massengill dissolved in water for a small dog, at least double that for a large. Soak the dog and let him marinate for about ten minutes, then shampoo and rinse. One can only muse on the true story behind the first application of douche to a dog.

THE CHEMIST-APPROVED RECIPE:

This formula originally appeared in *Chemical and Engineering News*, a publication of the American Chemical Society:

    4 cups (1.1 liters) 3% hydrogen peroxide
    4 tablespoons baking soda
    1 teaspoon liquid dishwashing soap

Wet the dog and saturate him with the mixture, keeping it away from his eyes. Let him marinate for five minutes at least, then rinse and shampoo. Chemists say that this formula causes a chemical reaction that breaks up the odor-causing sulfur compounds in a skunk's spray, while the soap dissolves the oily component of the spray. Don't store this remedy though. It can explode!

NATURAL FLEA CONTROL

🐾 Use a fine-toothed flea comb to remove fleas from your dog. Dip the comb into a bowl of hot soapy water after each sweep; this will kill the fleas.

🐾 Thorough vacuuming is a potent aid in flea control to capture fleas in the environment as well as flea eggs. Fleas spend a large part of their time off their hosts. Pay special attention to the dog's bed area and any dark, damp spots, where fleas are likely to lay their eggs. Seal the vacuum cleaner bag and dispose of it away from the house, or burn it. Wash your pet's bed in hot soapy water, and dry it in a hot dryer or in the sunshine.

🐾 Try rinsing your pet with water in which a couple tablespoons of an insect repellent oil, such as pennyroyal oil or tea tree oil, have been dissolved. Do not apply these oils directly to your pet's skin—full strength is too strong.

🐾 D-limonene, a citrus by-product, is also a useful flea repellent. Steep two sliced lemons in 2 cups (475 ml) of boiling water. Let the mixture steep over night, then use it as a rinse after bathing your dog, or sponge the mixture onto the dog. Do not rinse it off.

🐾 Diatomaceous earth, a powdered chalky substance that is the fossilized remains of diatoms, or one-celled algae, is also effective against fleas. The earth breaks down lipids in the chitinous coating that forms the flea's exoskeleton, dehydrating and killing the flea. Diatomaceous earth is safe to use as a flea powder on your pet; you can also dust it into furniture, rugs, floor cracks, and crevices.

🐾 Brewer's yeast can be used as a dietary supplement (1 tablespoon for a large dog), or as a natural flea powder. Zinc supplements are helpful: try a 10 mg tablet per day for a small dog and 20 mg for a large dog.

SOME MEDICAL ALERTS

Do not give your dog ibuprofen or acetaminophen for pain. Both can cause kidney damage or gastric ulcers in dogs. A baby aspirin is usually safe, but in general, it is dangerous to give over-the-counter human medications to dogs. Drug toxicity from human medications administered by owners is one of the most common types of canine poisoning.

BLOAT

Gastric dilatation-volvulus, commonly referred to as bloat, is a medical emergency. The dog's stomach fills with gas and fluid and then twists upon its long axis, shutting off blood supply to vital organs. The dog goes into shock and 25 percent of dogs that have a severe incidence of bloat die. Bloat is more common in large, deep-chested breeds; in a Purdue University study, breeds found to have the highest incidence were the Great Dane, Akita, bloodhound, Weimaraner, standard poodle, and setters. Symptoms include restlessness, pacing, a distended stomach, rapid panting, unproductive retching, and thick "ropy" salivation. Although some owners have helped a bloating dog by passing a stomach tube, this can be dangerous and do more harm than good. Because bloat can kill quickly, the best thing to do is get your dog to a veterinarian as soon as possible. Risk factors for bloat include breed, increased age, dogs who are fed large amounts of dry kibble once a day, rapid eating, raised food bowls, dogs who exercise just after eating, and genetic predisposition (close relative who bloated). Bloat also tends to recur. If your dog is at risk for bloat, divide his food ration into several meals. Do not feed from a raised bowl and purchase an "antibloat" dog bowl—they have raised projections that force the dog to work around them to get all the food, slowing the pace at which the dog eats. Don't exercise your dog or allow him to be too active right after a meal. If your dog has bloated in the past, know the phone number and location of the nearest 24 hour vet hospital! For dogs at a very high risk, some vets perform a "prophylactic gastropexy," where the stomach is stitched to the abdominal wall.

HEATSTROKE

All dogs are susceptible to heatstroke, especially geriatric dogs, but the brachiocephalic, or short-nosed, dog breeds, such as the old English bulldog, pug, Pekingese, Boston terrier, bullmastiff, shih tzu, and Pomeranian are the most likely to develop heat prostration or breathing problems during hot, humid weather. As a result of their foreshortened facial conformation, these breeds have palates that can get sucked into the tracheal opening when they pant heavily, obstructing

breathing. In some cases, this defect can be corrected surgically. These breeds also have trouble swimming because of their breathing difficulties and should never be left alone near a pool. If your dog becomes overheated, move it to shade and direct a fan on to the dog. Do NOT use ice or ice water to reduce the dog's body temperature. Ice can cause the superficial blood vessels to constrict, essentially trapping body heat! Cool, not cold, tap water is better. Soak a towel in cool tap water and wrap the dog

in the cool towel. Rubbing alcohol can be used on the stomach, then a fan can be used to hasten evaporation. After your dog's body temperature has been lowered, he should be taken to a veterinarian even if he seems better. Heat prostration affects all of the body's systems, so it is a prudent idea to have the dog checked for lingering effects.

COPING WITH A
HIGH-ENERGY DOG

Before acquiring a dog, you need to realize that you cannot force a high-energy dog to be a couch potato. It won't work. High energy dogs—typically the sporting breeds, terriers, malamutes, and huskies—inevitably require exercise and mental stimulation, or they will become destructive and neurotic. Think before you get a dog. There are plenty of dog breeds with lower energy levels. That said, there are some suggestions for helping your dog burn off some of its energy.

ROAD WORK: Jogging along with your dog on a leash is best, but if that is not possible, there are hitches designed to safely attach dogs to a bicycle, allowing you to bicycle along at a moderate pace on a safe path with the dog trotting along beside. Dogs can also be trained to use a treadmill (under supervision).

DOG DAY CARE: Even just a couple of days a week are a help! Yes, it costs money, but consider the alternative—a ruined home and unhappy dogs. If there are no nearby day-care options, hire a daily dog walker.

PLAY YARDS: Instead of banishing your dog to a barren yard, or a yard that contains nothing but places he's supposed to stay away from, construct a play yard with dog toys or an obstacle or agility course, and teach your dog how to use it. Even zoos have learned that animals require an interesting environment for mental health. However, make sure that the play yard is safe.

COMPANIONS: In many ways, two dogs are easier than one. Two dogs can wrestle together happily for hours, and your dog will not have to depend on you and you alone for companionship.

STRUCTURE: Most dogs will learn that there are "on" and "off" periods during their day. If they know they can expect a good stiff walk or a run in the park at the beginning and end of their day, they will learn to be patient and wait during the "off" times. The key here is structure. Dogs have excellent internal clocks. They will be calmer if they know they can expect an exercise period at a regular time.

MENTAL STIMULATION: Obedience classes, agility classes, tracking dog classes, and lure coursing are all activities that will provide your dog mental stimulation, which is important in keeping your dog happy. Remember that a dog that isn't stimulated mentally often becomes a destructive dog.

INTRIGUING TOYS HIDDEN AROUND THE HOUSE: Stuff large marrow bones with cheese spread, peanut butter, or another treat, then freeze them. Just before you leave, hide one or two of these around the house. Finding the bones and ferreting out the "marrow" will occupy your dog and help him through the "separation hump" when you leave.

DOMINANCE
RESTRUCTURING

Dogs are pack animals that act in accordance with their understanding of a hierarchical pack structure. Behavior problems can arise according to how the dog perceives its place in the human household, or pack. Low-ranking dogs that show problems related to submission and lack of self-confidence (such as submissive urination or separation anxiety) need to have their self-confidence bolstered. High-ranking dogs with problems related to seeing themselves as the alpha member of the pack (possessiveness over objects, growling, nipping, aggressive, or resentful response to a reasonable command) need to learn that the owner is alpha.

While all dogs benefit from tactful obedience training, adjust the tenor of the training to the nature of the dog. Severe cases of submissiveness or dominance are best dealt with in partnership with a dog behavior consultant, but here are a few hints.

SHOWING WHO'S BOSS

For a dominant dog, obedience training should be structured and matter of fact. Do not overpraise the dog for simple things. Do not let a dominant dog showing aggressive behavior patterns to initiate play. Dominant dogs conduct "play" sessions with their human according to the dog's rules, reinforcing the dog's idea that he is dominant. Play sessions with a dominant dog should be started by the human, and the human should set the rules. The dog should respond to your commands. Have him sit, and only when he does throw a ball. If he will not return the ball, make the dog return it (without being confrontational), even if you have to tug him to you on a leash. If the dog becomes overexcited or aggressive during the play session, stop the play with the curt word "enough."

Do not play wrestling-type games with a dominant dog. If you play tug-of-war, make sure you win. By the same token, avoid setting up a confrontation with a dominant dog, lest you lose.

THE NEW WINNER

When training a submissive dog, set up situations that allow the dog to succeed and be sure that you do not overcorrect. At the same time, do not encourage the submissive dog's anxieties by treating the dog in an overemotional manner. When you return home, greet the dog quietly, and keep your departures just as low key. With a submissive dog, it is a good idea to play tug-of-war and ALLOW the dog to win.

---

3 STEPS TO TAKE FOR A SNAKE BITE

If a snake bites your dog, he will need veterinary help quickly. Follow the points below—they will give you the greatest chance of saving your dog's life:

If you can, identify the snake or note its markings—but only do so without putting yourself in danger.

Carry your dog to your vehicle. Try to keep him as quiet as possible to help avoid spreading the snake's venom.

If available, use a phone to call your veterinary practice to alert it about the emergency before you arrive.

NOTE: *Applying a tourniquet is controversial because if applied incorrectly the leg can become gangrenous and need amputating.*

WHEN TO SEE YOUR VET

By taking care of your dog's health, you are giving him the best chance of a longer, more comfortable life. Make sure that you are aware of the early signs of illness, and seek advice as soon as a potential problem arises.

EARLY SIGNS OF ILLNESS

If you notice one or more of the following symptoms in your dog, it may be a sign of a problem. Be sure to bring your dog to a veterinarian for a checkup:

Decreased appetite
Weight loss
Changes in behavior
Changes in activity levels
Less interaction with family
   members and other pets in
   the household
Episodes of confusion or
   disorientation
A change in sleeping patterns,
   such as sleeping too much
   or difficulty sleeping
Heightened thirst
Increased urination
Changes in housebreaking habits
More frequent bowel movements
   or constipation
Bad breath/red gums

Difficulty eating/chewing
Excessive panting or changes in
   breathing patterns/coughing
Collapse, fainting, or signs
   of weakness
Seizures
Tremors or shaking episodes
Difficulty climbing stairs or
   jumping up
Poor vision or hearing
New lumps or bumps

VACCINATIONS

Discuss with your veterinarian which vaccinations and boosters are appropriate for your dog and how often. Among the ones to consider are those for distemper, hepatitis, leptospirosis, and parvovirus. Depending on where you live, some vaccines, such as rabies, are mandatory.

GERIATRIC CHECKUPS

As your dog gets older, it will need more appointments with a veterinarian for checkups, preferably twice a year. Many veterinarians now offer an initial checkup for older dogs, sometimes referred to as a "geriatric" screening. When this screening takes place will depend on your dog's size and breed.

GIVING A LIFT

If you need to lift an older dog that can no longer jump up into your vehicle, bend down from your knees to a comfortable height, and place your left arm around the front of the dog's body. Then place your other arm around the dog's hindquarters. Gently lift up the dog, allowing the weight of its body to rest on your arms. Don't let your dog hang down—this can injure the dog. You can invest in a special ramp that allows your dog to walk from the ground into the vehicle.

HEALTHY LIVING PLAN FOR THE OLDER DOG

1. Arrange a veterinary checkup for an older dog at least twice a year.
2. Adjust your dog's diet to an appropriate portion to prevent obesity. If your dog is overweight, discuss a weight-loss program with its veterinarian.
3. Provide protection from the weather.
4. Play with your pet—mental alertness is important to its health.
5. Groom your dog regularly and use this time to look for any swellings.
6. Provide your dog with regular daily exercise—avoid the occasional marathon hike, which could be more harmful than beneficial for your dog.
7. Keep your dog's vaccinations up-to-date.
8. Be sure that any medication is given regularly.
9. If you notice a change in your pet's behavior, seek veterinary advice.
10. Keep your dog away from situations in which a conflict can occur. Older dogs are at greater risk of being injured than younger ones.

INDEX

PICTURE CREDITS:
Inside pages: Shutterstock®; *The Dog Book* published by T. Fisher Unwin (1898); *Our Friend the Dog* published by Dean and Son; *The Dog* published by Cassell, Petter, and Galpin.

The Healthy Living Plan for Older Dogs and other advice found in When to See Your Vet is used courtesy of David Alderton, from his book *Young at Heart* (2005).